INNER WORDS

for every day of the year

chosen and arranged by Emmy Arnold

THE PLOUGH PUBLISHING HOUSE

Woodcrest, Rifton, New York

From the writings of Johann Christoph Blumhardt, Christoph Blumhardt, Dietrich Bonhoeffer, Bodelschwingh, Eberhard Arnold, and others.

Printed by
Lansing-Broas Printing Co., Inc.
1963

© Copyright 1963

In choosing these "Inner Words" for every day of the year, I thought especially of those who have an ear to listen. This hour of the world, with its need, its destructiveness and sin, is so serious that we must hear voices of our time which speak to men's hearts. It has been most important to me in choosing these words that they come from men who have not only expressed their faith in words, but who have actually lived what they thought and wrote and believed.

For those who have not known my husband, Eberhard Arnold, I want to say briefly that he fought for a living faith in Jesus. He dedicated his entire life (1883-1935) to this fight in a very practical way. For years he was closely connected with the Christian youth movement in Germany. In those years he and I were part of a group of people who often met in our home in Berlin in a search for a new, genuine way of life. A few of these people felt together the very strong urge to live together in the spirit of the early Christians, who put everything aside to follow Christ. Wanting to live in complete community of goods and of life, Eberhard and I and our children with some others began in 1920 a very simple life in complete sharing as those who want to follow Jesus. This life in community, constantly born anew, has continued. It has gone through much joy, but also sorrow and struggle, for forty-two years. To such living communities, wherever they are, to the spirit they want to serve, I wish to dedicate this little booklet.

EMMY ARNOLD

January 1

Jesus brought new tidings into this world —the message of another order of all things. For the present world order this message means judgment and revolution of the whole of life. This message concerns the coming reign of God, which must bring to an end the present age with its glorification of man.

EBERHARD ARNOLD, *The Early Christians*

January 2

Without God the age sinks down into emptiness and lovelessness, into self-will and self-delusion. The revelation of the love of the Father is shown forth in Jesus.

EBERHARD ARNOLD, *The Early Christians*

January 3

It is well for us that at such hours the light is shining from the stable of Bethlehem, and that we are able to sense what it means that the kingdom of God was born as a little child when the time was fulfilled.

EBERHARD ARNOLD, *Advent 1928*

January 4

The newborn Christ-Child had to be taken away from the land of His birth very soon. He had to flee from Herod the king so that He might be saved for something greater, yes, for the cross!

EBERHARD ARNOLD, from a letter, Dec. 1933

January 5

The testimony of my life is always only for the One through whom we live and have all things. This testimony, however, requires unity with the Church of Christ.

EBERHARD ARNOLD, from a letter, Nov. 1919

January 6

The wise men from the Orient had heard the Word speaking within them, and seen it shining without; and so they came to the Christ who was not born yet, though He was already born in their hearts.

EBERHARD ARNOLD, *Innenland*, "The Living Word"

January 7

Every heart that is filled with God's goodness reveals Christ's humility and the patience of His love.

> EBERHARD ARNOLD, *Innenland*,
> "The Living Word"

January 8

In Jesus, God's image appeared with utmost clarity and finality. Henceforth it is from Jesus that man's calling comes into our hearts. The image of God which He brings us is love.

> EBERHARD ARNOLD, *Innenland*,
> "The Inner Life"

January 9

In this birth, God pours His light so freely into the soul that in man's nature and being a great fullness of light is given, which presses outwards and overflows into powers, and even into the physical man.

> ECKEHART, 1260-1327

January 10

The will which lives in the light repels the attacks of the darkness.

> EBERHARD ARNOLD, *Innenland*,
> "The Experience of God"

Christ, the coming Lord of the eternal world of light, reveals himself in His wonderful light as the Spirit of His Church.

EBERHARD ARNOLD, *Innenland*,
"Light and Fire"

January 11

The meaning of darkness can be exposed only in the light. Darkness is revealed only when the light does away with it. Unless the darkness is removed, there is no knowledge of the source of light. The reception of light brings liberating redemption. Forgiveness is the removal of the darkening powers of night.

EBERHARD ARNOLD, *Innenland*,
"Light and Fire"

January 12

He who wants to fight against death and devil must not be afraid of wounds.

BODELSCHWINGH, Director of Bethel
(an institute for the handicapped),
who resisted Hitler

January 13

God created this world and placed us in

this world, and hid the other world from us; and we are told very seriously, "Do your duty in the things you see! *There* you must be truthful, there be just, there seek the spirit and not the form; there you will experience God's glory." This creation in its physical existence which is now covered over with death and infamy, shall experience this glory in what God does to those who love Him.

CHRISTOPH BLUMHARDT, "Thoughts of Advent"

January 14

It is possible that the fruit of our prayers will be experienced only by later generations. They can then break out into songs of praise such as we ourselves would so much like to be able to send up to heaven in thanks for the answers to our prayers. How many blows are needed before the walls of a well-fortified city are broken down! Our prayers are hammer blows on the bulwarks of the Prince of darkness; they have to be repeated often. Many years can go by, yes, many generations can pass away before a breach is made.

JOHANN CHRISTOPH BLUMHARDT, *Blumhardt Calendar for the Year 1962*

January 15

One thing, and one only, carries men through all that is difficult—the love of Christ, which urges and gives strength. It is not our love to Christ and perhaps not even Christ's love to us personally, but His love to poor, ruined sinners such as we are. Much water will not extinguish this love; the floods will not drown it. Pray that this love may rule our lives!

HUDSON TAYLOR

January 16

The only conqueror in the world is Jesus Christ. For Him we must make room. In Him we must live and move and have our being. For Him we must fight by repentance and contrition for our own nature, by sacrificing what is our own, even the best that is in us. When we surrender ourselves body and soul, not keeping anything of our own nature—that is what will help toward His victory. He is the true victor! Thank God, we know this. The kingdom of God is in His hands.

CHRISTOPH BLUMHARDT, *Blumhardt Calendar*

January 17

It matters little what form of prayer we adopt or how many words we use, what matters is the faith which lays hold on God and touches the heart of the Father who knew us long before we came to Him. Genuine prayer is never "good works", an exercise or a pious attitude, but it is always the prayer of a child to a Father.

DIETRICH BONHOEFFER, *The Cost of Discipleship*

January 18

In many, I see how again and again there come shadows and low points in deeds and acts, in spite of luminous heights. Then there is simply the faith, the readiness to receive and hold on to Jesus Christ, who alone is the One we need.

EBERHARD ARNOLD, from a letter, Jan. 1927

January 19

I have the faith for you and for us all that we are going on the way of community in God's love.

EBERHARD ARNOLD, from a letter, Jan. 1926

January 20

Not our inadequacy, but God's perfect will is now the substance of our life and thinking. Therefore, from now on our entire interest goes away from ourselves, toward all people of the earth and of all worlds of God, toward near and far creatures of God; toward those who have died and those unborn. The interest of God's kingdom embraces the times and spaces of all worlds of God, of the earth as well as of all other worlds with all their spiritual princes and creatures of light. That God's kingdom may become reality on earth as it is real in heaven—that is what we have to live for. Certainly, for this a turning is necessary.

EBERHARD ARNOLD, from a letter, July 1934

January 21

A turning is necessary; but anyone who would remain at the point of turning is not usable for the kingdom of God. The decisive thing is to see God's kingdom, to enter God's kingdom.

EBERHARD ARNOLD, from a letter, July 1934

January 22

As educators, you need the daily leading of the spirit of light which immediately recognizes, attacks and does away with all darkening elements, even before they can come to rule over the little sensitive souls.

> EBERHARD ARNOLD, from a letter, Feb. 1934

January 23

God's Word falls into the hearts of mortal and erring men, to pervade them from the very roots with the divine Spirit and the Christian life.

> EBERHARD ARNOLD, *Innenland*, "The Living Word"

Only the spirit of the perfect life has the power to overcome death.

> EBERHARD ARNOLD, *Innenland*, "The Holy Spirit"

January 24

By what can one recognize the emotional nature? The emotional nature never gives a witness.

> EBERHARD ARNOLD, from a letter, July 1934

How wonderful is God's grace, when all depression and fearfulness give way to the joy which inspires us with the childlike trust in the unity and leading of Christ's Spirit.

> EBERHARD ARNOLD, from a letter, June 1934

January 25

The first steps toward resurrection are taken when believers are no longer concerned with themselves, but turn completely and solely to the great cause of God's kingdom.

> EBERHARD ARNOLD, from a letter, July 1934

January 26

To experience the totality of those who believe in Christ as one organism, as one body, as the Body of Christ, is a special experience of faith. With this Body we are indissolubly united; its life is our life, its deficiency is our deficiency, its weakness is our weakness, its strength is our strength.

> EBERHARD ARNOLD, "The Body of Christ"

January 27

I entreat God for unambiguous clarity of expression, certainty and decision of word, comprehensive attestation to the whole Gospel. And all this not through intellectual calculation and with a mental aim, but in the strength of what is given by God himself, and through inspiration.

> EBERHARD ARNOLD, "Christ and
> His Church"

January 28

It is by no means a matter of indifference how I myself or my hand, just as other selves and other hands, are being used. The greatness that fills and surrounds my smallness and other smallnesses wants to use everything, even the most insignificant, for its service, if only it is ready to be used in the right proportion.

> EBERHARD ARNOLD, from a letter,
> Nov. 1934

January 29

Be a fanatic for Christ; then you will also have community with me. The repentance which works daily amongst us is simply an overpowering conviction of the malice and vanity of all that we are and do in our own strength; so that the concepts of pride and humility simply cease to be and one thing alone remains: grace.

EBERHARD ARNOLD, from a letter, Sept. 1921

January 30

There is a certainty in which we accept —really take—that for which we have asked. But this is possible only when the Spirit himself can fully speak within us. God speaks when we are silent. His will becomes powerful when our self-will becomes quiet. His power is evident when our weakness no longer is "strength".

EBERHARD ARNOLD, from a letter, July 1922

January 31

And now I must tell you about the sun. The sun shines. He sends forth his beams and gives warmth. He awakens and strengthens life. Should he disappear, everything would suddenly be dead, really dead! But it is not one and the same thing whether the sun shines on a rock or on a flower. Certainly the sun has also awakened life from rocks. In hearts of stone that will not be called to life, the light of God works in a different way than in a heart that receives the light.

EBERHARD ARNOLD, from a letter, July 1922

February 1

The light shines on every human being that comes to this world. But only he who accepts it completely, and only as long as he accepts it completely, will receive power, strength and tasks.

EBERHARD ARNOLD, from a letter, July 1922

February 2

The fact that we experience something is not what matters; whom and what we experience is alone decisive. Who God is and what He wills and does should become so great and exclusive that through it we forget the experience itself, that is, ourselves and our experience, and lose sight of it completely. The greatest experience completely reveals our own insignificance.

Eberhard Arnold, from a letter, Easter 1934

February 3

It is frightening and depressing when religion is misused to enslave and to rob the soul of its every freedom. How often does this happen! Nearly always and everywhere. It is the same with love. The noblest, purest and most divine becomes the lowest and meanest and most perishable, through the demonic powers that are released when this one area becomes a law to itself. God is freedom, deliverance from all slavery. We remain true to this watch-word. It becomes ever clearer to me that all unfreedom is of the devil.

Eberhard Arnold, from a letter, Feb. 1925

February 4

The kingdom of God cannot be simply a future state. Certainly for the vast majority it lies still in the future. Yet each one of us should seek to become united in the Church of Jesus Christ. We must begin to get free, so that at least amongst those of us who have come to a mutual understanding, anxieties will cease. Then we can also give thanks, and in thanking God, ask and pray. When we ask, we must have a firm foundation. We know where we stand, and the ground upon which we are founded is firm. Our community is to be stronger than the gates of death and of hell, so that we can fight and work upon the earth for the coming of our future kingdom, our kingdom of God.

CHRISTOPH BLUMHARDT, "Joy in the Lord"

February 5

Everything you do, and how you do it, must show the one clear image which reveals the full love of Christ. Without a daily coming together, there can be no life in marriage or in the Church.

EBERHARD ARNOLD, from a letter, Nov. 1934

February 6

I am certain that we are facing our true task, which is very great and powerful. What we need is always one and the same, no matter what we call it: the baptism of the Spirit—perfect love—the works of purity and truth—Jesus Christ!

> EBERHARD ARNOLD, from a letter, July 1922

February 7

Those truths of the spirit's struggle are best experienced in life itself. In the steadfast constancy of faith, which is the fighting spirit itself, one then says "Yes" to this out of one's heart. For this fight is indeed the highest love itself, as we know from Blumhardt and above all from the crucified One himself.

> EBERHARD ARNOLD, from a letter, Sept. 1931

February 8

The community of redeemed sinners becomes an instrument and tool of the fighting spirit, an instrument which fights compromise without monasticism and without cowardice; through forgiveness it creates the atmosphere for a life as God wills it.

> EBERHARD ARNOLD, from a letter, Sept. 1931

February 9

The heirs of the old covenant of unity, in dedication to Christ, extend the work of peace over the whole earth. For all land belongs to God. Jesus has shed the glowing heat of His rule of peace from the other world into the world of men.

EBERHARD ARNOLD, *Innenland*,
"The Peace of God"

February 10

The lighting up of God's countenance in Jesus Christ gives this peace which is the deepest peace of the heart. As national peace it is justice, and as international peace it is love to one's enemies.

EBERHARD ARNOLD, *Innenland*,
"The Peace of God"

February 11

Is it still possible today to bring the true Gospel to men? Is it possible once again to experience the new man in Christ? Most people have given up this hope. Yet even if the whole world no longer believes in the new man in Christ, we must believe.

Christ wants to create men here on earth. Before He came, people could also die saved; people also had comfort and life and death before Christ came. But Jesus came to create new men full of the power of eternal life. These men are to have within them the love of God.

CHRISTOPH BLUMHARDT, *Blumhardt Calendar*

February 12

If we would follow Jesus we must take certain definite steps. The first step, which follows the call, cuts the disciple off from his previous existence. The call to follow at once produces a new situation. To stay in the old situation makes discipleship impossible ... The first step places the disciple in the situation where faith is possible. If he refuses to follow and stays behind, he does not learn how to believe. He who is called must go out of his situation in which he cannot believe, into the situation in which, first and foremost, faith is possible.

DIETRICH BONHOEFFER, *The Cost of Discipleship*

February 13

If God blesses His people with peace, one may not think alone of the peace of the soul, and just as little may one think only of international peace. Peace with God brings about the new order of a kingdom of peace which enforces itself both inwardly and outwardly.

> EBERHARD ARNOLD, *Innenland*,
> "The Peace of God"

February 14

Let us ask the Lord to create the faith that expects and entreats something of the Savior! This faith is needed in our time. Only with this faith shall we achieve anything great; with this faith we can overcome the powers of darkness. Only with this faith which sighs to heaven shall we save thousands; only with this faith shall we draw God's powers down from above, so that the wretched may find life and abundance.

> JOHANN CHRISTOPH BLUMHARDT,
> *Blumhardt Calendar*

February 15

There need to be people who knock and who go on knocking until heaven is opened. All of you are knockers as soon as you ask: Father in heaven, visit us anew with mercy from heaven; for we cannot get along unless powers from above again come down to us.

JOHANN CHRISTOPH BLUMHARDT,
Blumhardt Calendar

February 16

Only by love can everything be overcome. Without love we find ourselves in a lifelong state of strife with ourselves and others, without achieving any result but weariness and finally pessimism or even misanthropy.

HILTY, *Blumhardt Calendar*

February 17

Our life will become not narrower, but broader; not more limited, but more boundless; not more regulated, but more abundant; not more pedantic, but more bounteous; not more sober, but more enthusiastic; not more faint-hearted, but more daring; not worse and more human, but filled with God and ever better; not sadder, but happier; not more incapable, but more creative. All this is Jesus and His Spirit of freedom! He is coming to us. Therefore let us forget. Let is forgive everyone, just as we must be forgiven everything, and go into the future radiant with joy!

EBERHARD ARNOLD, from a letter, July 1922

February 18

Paul does not say we should ask for the removal of temptations, but only that we should not allow them to rule over us. The only thing a Christian has to watch is that temptations do not overpower him, that he does not give way to them, as long as for the time being he cannot come to the point where they are taken away from him by God's power. Here a man must prove to be patient and faithful, and if he is, much relief and help can come to him from the Lord.

JOHANN CHRISTOPH BLUMHARDT, *Questions of Faith*

February 19

Our faith is not tied to a dogma; it binds us to the one God who is God to all men.

Whether you call yourself Christian or Mohammedan, you are just as much God's as I am. You Gentile and you Jew are just as much God's as I am, for you are all men. You are a man and should be proud of it, because this comes from God. You should not be proud of your religion, because this comes from men. My body and my life come from God. Do my books and my teachings come from God? No indeed! Only what I have of Jesus comes from God.

CHRISTOPH BLUMHARDT, "People of Zion"

February 20

Ask that you may have a joyful heart and a joyful soul, especially towards other people. Ask that your joyful, loving heart may not fail you when you encounter an enemy. For how will you overcome the enemy? By your fist or by words of abuse? How will you go forward then to a great new time of which all men are a part? How are things to improve unless all come to this new time? If you condemn and judge, nothing can improve. God's people cannot make anything better if they act like the rest of the world, if they wage war and pick quarrels and fall again and again into all kinds of mistrust of people. No, truly, our salvation must produce a new morality; then we will be able to love even those who hate us.

CHRISTOPH BLUMHARDT, *Blumhardt Calendar*

February 21

Don't think that people are unbelieving. They are not unbelieving, they are only tormented. I have stopped speaking about unbelief, though here and there one can do so. But in general, please don't call people unbelievers; instead call them tormented! They cannot open their eyes; they are drunk with their misery; they are satiated with their suffering; they do not see out through the veils. Say to them what one will—saying does not help much.

CHRISTOPH BLUMHARDT, *Blumhardt Calendar*

February 22

You are God's helpers, and you will perish miserably if you do not want to help.

Long enough you have called on the Savior for His help. He has done His duty from the beginning. You need not remind Him. Now it is *your* turn to stand by Him and to do something to help *Him!*

CHRISTOPH BLUMHARDT, "The Light of the World"

February 23

God grant that all the old piousness may soon fall to pieces, so that Christ can be fulfilled. "I have come not to abolish the law and the prophets, but to fulfil them." If Jesus said this, then I ask, how is this to be fulfilled today? How are you fulfilling it? If anyone says, "I can't do it," then he is a liar. You can be meek, you can be self-denying, you can be kind and patient, you can control yourself. If you cannot, then be quiet about your faith and your piety. We can do everything! Though it will not come all at once, yet in time we can do more and more, and finally everything. God be praised and thanked that this is so!

CHRISTOPH BLUMHARDT, *Blumhardt Calendar*

February 24

God wants to give an indestructible harmony to the inner life of the heart, which outwardly will be active in life as a mighty melody of love. This is the power to be active which comes from the energy of inner concentration. Concentration in the heart leads to a gathering of a people in whose activity and work the kingdom of God can be recognized as righteousness, peace and joy in the Holy Spirit.

EBERHARD ARNOLD, *Innenland*

February 25

The extreme confusion which has come over all the countries and peoples of the world must be transformed by the power from the inmost spring into a realm and a nation wherein peace has deeply penetrated, and where the powers of the coming kingdom of God are poured out through the Holy Spirit.

EBERHARD ARNOLD

February 26

We are reborn through the living Word of God and through the moving Spirit of Jesus Christ. The strength and might of

God does not live in pale recollection. It does not work in dead learning. The Word of truth which brings forth the new life must ever anew show itself to be living and powerful in our hearts, if our spirit is not to fall a prey to death.

> EBERHARD ARNOLD, *Innenland*,
> "The Experience of God"

February 27

The root of life is the spirit of joy which starts to grow when life is kindled. When the soul is fired by the Holy Spirit, then it triumphs in the body; a great flame of new life leaps up.

> EBERHARD ARNOLD, *Innenland*,
> "Light and Fire"

February 28

Glowing light shines o'er the Chaos,
And that light redeems in judgment,
The Sun is ris'n, the Sun is ris'n.

Peace now smiles, joy purifies,
Spirit heals, Truth unites,
The day is here, the day is here.

Prison yields, harsh chains fall,
Freedom binding, jubilation!
The Lord now reigns, the Lord now reigns.

EBERHARD ARNOLD, Sannerz 1922

February 29

We wait for the eternal light
To come into our midst this night;
We wait expectant, silent.
Our hearts are poor and barren soil.
O, love of God, pity us all
And in this hour be present.

Light streams down from eternity,
And, finding hearts open and free,
Dispelleth all the darkness.
The fears of night have fled away,
God's Spirit comes as unity
And faith now leads and guides us.

TRUDI HUESSY, 1928

March 1

The inner source of strength, which in silent stillness lets God himself speak and work, leads the believer from the decline of death to the dawn of life. This life forces its way outwards in the stream of creative spirit, and yet cannot lose itself in the outer world.

>   Eberhard Arnold, *Innenland*,
>   "The Inner Life"

March 2

Unless we share the need and guilt of the world, we fall a prey to untruthfulness and lifelessness, to eternal and physical death.

>   Eberhard Arnold, *Innenland*,
>   "The Inner Life"

March 3

Into what depths of misery did Christ not have to go! And how gloriously He was led out of them! Yet all this took place for our sake. Just as He, in the midst of the torments of the cross, still remained the beloved of God, the Child of the Father, so we too remain the beloved of the Lord, His children. We remain this all the more if we suffer like Him, we remain this no matter how much affliction may come upon us.

>   Johann Christoph Blumhardt,
>   *Blumhardt Calendar*

March 4

This is quite certain: those who know God, who honor and trust Him, those who depend on Him as their dear God and Father with a pure unblemished faith, are assured of our God's comforting promise. And what God promises, be it temporal or eternal, He keeps and gives faithfully.

MARTIN LUTHER

March 5

To pray and supplicate in everything means simply this: to stand before the Lord prayerfully always, day and night, whether standing up or lying down, walking or sitting, working or resting, at all times, in every situation, in whatever I am doing. It must be clearly understood that my prayer goes to God, that I imagine the Savior to be present and that I never lose sight of Him. I must do everything under His eyes and turn my glance to Him at all times. This is how we pray "in everything".

JOHANN CHRISTOPH BLUMHARDT,
Questions of Faith

March 6

Fire lays waste and kills all that is consecrated to death, all forces of envy. Fire consumes.

The spirit of unity is the light of God that comes down from heaven, most deeply and inwardly akin to the glory of all suns.

EBERHARD ARNOLD, *Innenland*,
"Light and Fire"

March 7

That which holds back the awakening life of spring is the deadness of winter. That which is against warmth is deadening coldness. That which is against uniting love brings about disintegrating death. Death threatens life. Between light and darkness there is enmity and war to the last.

EBERHARD ARNOLD, *Innenland*,
"Light and Fire"

March 8

The springtime of the climbing sun alone could bring over the earth and all its inhabitants the sunny time, the longed-for, expected time, which alone can awaken life, strong, prolific and abiding life. At the end of the days, light was to triumph over darkness. The final springtime of all worlds and of all ages was one day to melt away the whole present age which is the cold, dead and dark wintertime, the deadening ice age of the present world, and do away with it for all time.

> EBERHARD ARNOLD, *Innenland*,
> "Light and Fire"

March 9

The fire that comes down from heaven is the blazing sign in which the God of the covenant draws near to men. For He is the creative Spirit of the central fire who created heaven and earth, sun, light and glowing warmth and all life.

> EBERHARD ARNOLD, *Innenland*,
> "Light and Fire"

March 10

Jesus came to light a sea of fire upon the earth. His whole will is set upon its burning. He is the last, the original unfallen man who alone, as the bearer of the flaming Spirit, can be the light bearer, the sustainer of glowing warmth and the kindler of fire.

His flame of the Spirit is the last possibility for becoming man, for union with God and for brotherly community.

> EBERHARD ARNOLD, *Innenland*,
> "Light and Fire"

March 11

The fire of God's light never appears without consuming judgment over what is old, over what is withered and dried up, over what is lifeless, unsocial and unjust, over all that has fallen a prey to death.

> EBERHARD ARNOLD, *Innenland*,
> "Light and Fire"

March 12

The important thing is not saying "Lord, Lord," but the inward truthfulness in which we do God's will. In fact we rejoice about all those who are open to this freedom and this will to love, even if they are not yet able to confess to Christ at all. A free movement, a movement of the spirit, an early Christian movement, an academic and modern movement needs the free working of all those who are called, and free personal responsibility.

> EBERHARD ARNOLD, from a letter,
> Feb. 1920

March 13

Yesterday we again had about a hundred people in our house. The Letter to the Romans, which is the affirmation of justice, and the question of group living in community of goods, was our agenda ... What we want is not an academic or student organization. We want personal, organic exchange between university people, middle-class and working-class people, who are moved by Christ and lead a free life of inward truthfulness and love.

> EBERHARD ARNOLD, from a letter, Jan. 1920

March 14

What is the purpose of our existence? The main thing is not to make sure that we are speedily saved. Anyone who thinks that is making a big mistake. The most important thing is to be fighters and to bring the world under God's feet. The main thing is that we should be the voice of justice on earth, and no longer tolerate the rule of sin and Satan. Then we are allied with God.

> CHRISTOPH BLUMHARDT, "God's Allies"

March 15

Jesus calls to His heroic way of most shameful death. The catastrophe of the final conflict must be provoked, because only thus can Satan with all his demonic powers be routed. Death on the cross is the decisive fact. It makes Jesus the unique leader of the new way, which is in accordance with the coming age of God. It makes Him the unique captain in the great conflict which achieves victory.

ERERHARD ARNOLD, *The Early Christians*

March 16

He who waits for God expects judgment and fire. In the judgment of fire the light of His salvation shines forth.

If your vision fails when you look at the sun, it is the fault of your eyes, not of the great light.

EBERHARD ARNOLD, *Innenland*, "Light and Fire"

March 17

In God's nearness, in the manifestation

of God's power, Jesus reveals our smallness and our antagonism more clearly than any human reasoning. God's light reveals everywhere to Him and to ourselves our baseness and smallness, our darkness and weakness. In His sight we can appear only as we really are.

EBERHARD ARNOLD, *Innenland*, "The Experience of God"

March 18

Through the death and resurrection of Christ a way has been broken for the body and flesh of men out of the lie of death into the truth of life . . . But this cannot come to be in the body and the flesh of lying and death, but in the body and flesh of truthfulness and of life. Therefore men must give their body and their flesh into the death of Jesus Christ as a sacrifice for the atonement of their guilt before God.

CHRISTOPH BLUMHARDT, "Thoughts of Advent"

March 19

Everybody must first go through the debt and guilt himself, before he can sense the truth in Jesus' resurrection and life. You do not go through the Savior and come to guilt; on the contrary, you must go through guilt and come to the Savior. Anyone who persuades himself that he can do it differently is on the wrong track. He cannot be prevented from making himself important in others' eyes with his faith; but the proof of the power and Spirit of Jesus Christ belongs only to the humble and beaten one who is ready to receive revelations of his guilt before expecting the revelation of his salvation.

> CHRISTOPH BLUMHARDT, "Thoughts of Advent"

March 20

Arise with joy, believe in Jesus, and you will be in the light. You will be saved, for this is the purpose of God's Son in His powerful love for you. Open your ears. Say, "Praise and thanks to God. God loves the world; now I too will be filled with love for everything that lives. Since Jesus, His Son, is only love, so I too will be only love. I can make myself a follower of this Son; therefore with Him I am of God; so I am loved and I love. Where there is love, there is life; and life is the light of men."

>   CHRISTOPH BLUMHARDT, *Blumhardt Calendar*

March 21

The mystery of the Church is Christ shining in her. He reveals His presence in the pure fire of the Holy Spirit. The clarity of His light tolerates no defilement. The mystery of the Church is the pure expectation of the coming of God's majesty in glory.

>   EBERHARD ARNOLD, *Innenland*, "Light and Fire"

March 22

In Christ's death, Christians die to wrath and its grim commands. A Christian is one who has died with Christ to all the elements of wrath. In Christ's Spirit, which is the love of God's heart, he is born a new man who lives in that different justice of loving patience.

>   EBERHARD ARNOLD, *Innenland*, "Light and Fire"

March 23

God opens hearts to final decision. In this decision we can make way for the light; we can lay aside all that is obscure as hated darkness; we can recognize and leave behind all dismal entanglement in guilt. All this we do in order to be renewed in the light of Jesus Christ to the life of His Church.

EBERHARD ARNOLD, *Innenland*, "Light and Fire"

March 24

If we are faithful in our hearts, then God will be able to make use of us even in times when things are not going so well for us. For we are called to work with Him, not against Him. Not only when we are joyful and gay can we do this, but also when we want to weep with God over the sins of the world. To make this easier for us, He sent His Son who was to bear the sins of the world in our midst. Him we can follow, and offer Him our shoulder to help carry the guilt.

CHRISTOPH BLUMHARDT, "People of Zion"

March 25

Unless we have opened eyes that hasten

toward the divine light, we are and remain blind.

In the perfect working of the light of the Spirit there lies concealed a power to eradicate and overcome evil which is stronger than all destructive forces.

EBERHARD ARNOLD, *Innenland*,
"Light and Fire"

March 26

Faith is a light of God that surpasses all human reason. The light of faith is nothing other than God drawing near and intervening. He who is in the sun has no lack of light.

EBERHARD ARNOLD, *Innenland*,
"Light and Fire"

March 27

The light is discoverer, liberator and leader. Wherever a life in God is brought about by the radiance of light within, wherever the inner and outer life meets Christ's radiant face, wherever His power puts an end to darkness, the guidance of all of life by the inner life begins.

EBERHARD ARNOLD, *Innenland*,
"Light and Fire"

March 28

His truth bears a new criterion which is decisive for the whole present age, a criterion which proves the purity and unity of the leading light. It is the unanimity of the Church of Christ of all ages.

EBERHARD ARNOLD, *Innenland*,
"Light and Fire"

The Church of Christ is the basis and ground of truth. It is a beacon, a light-star of justice.

PETER RIDEMAN, 16th century

March 29

Jesus steps in firmly where no one ever ventured before Him. The miserable come to the light for the first time and so do the sick, those whose spirits are confused, the whole mass of people for whom human society has no use. Jesus steps in amongst the despised, the enslaved, those who are looked down upon. He comes to those who are ignored by the educated people who have created an abyss between educated and uneducated, between rich and poor, between high and low. Jesus intervenes on the level of those who are ignored by the history of the nations and of society. These miserable people who have never come to the light are the very ones whose side Jesus takes.

> CHRISTOPH BLUMHARDT, "Jesus Among the Wretched"

March 30

I consider it very important that we who understand the striving and longing of today's religious-minded young people, meet for a thorough discussion. At Whitsuntide this year there must be a meeting where the most varied groups of the Christian movement come together, of the movement which comprises all nature and love of mankind.

> EBERHARD ARNOLD, from a letter, Sept. 1920

March 31

The message of the Gospel is resurrection from death. The Spirit of the risen Christ wants to kindle new fire, so as to establish life community anew, with the watchword,

"Light the candles! The Lord is truly risen!"

> EBERHARD ARNOLD, *Innenland*,
> "Light and Fire"

April 1

Whoever receives the spirit of the new creation which hastens on the end of all time, receives the eternal powers of the one God, who formed the first creation in the same spirit. The future strength of God, in its all-transforming expectation of the end, lives as the spirit of strength in the present aging creation. The new dawn has begun in it already. Everyone must see—a new creation is arising! Its Gospel is meant for every creature.

> EBERHARD ARNOLD, *Innenland*,
> "The Holy Spirit"

April 2

The garden must be won back for God. God himself will conquer and rule it. But men must be ready to accept this rule of God. The kingdom of God has the same earthly sound, the same earth-color, as the vanished paradise. Sin, the destroyer, which has kept us from rejoicing fully in the earth, must be overcome. Not man, renewed by God, but the enemy of God must leave the earth.

EBERHARD ARNOLD, "Jesus and the Future State"

April 3

With the hands of our souls we must hold firmly His burning light, because it wants to penetrate the graves. Nothing else can we have in our hands but His radiant life, because it conquers all worlds of death.

EBERHARD ARNOLD, *Innenland*

April 4

Perfect community is a matter of new birth and resurrection. Into our time also, the Holy Spirit of Jesus Christ has placed the power of eternal birth and new resurrection.

EBERHARD ARNOLD, *Innenland*, "The Holy Spirit"

April 5

Like the water of the mountains, the Spirit of the heights seeks the lowest place.

He strives downwards. His Church bears the lowly and childlike spirit which alone is of God. She is with Mary in the stable. The Church comes into being with Christ on the gallows. She goes the way of apostolic poverty. With her one mind and one heart, she honors no one but God in Christ Jesus.

> EBERHARD ARNOLD, *Innenland*,
> "The Holy Spirit"

April 6

The reality of repentance and of our smallness is effective only if one takes the smallness for granted. As long as that which moves us is not God and His kingdom but instead "my" heart, "my" inadequacy, "my" remorse and "my" repentance, the whole thing is and remains a completely heathen idolatry.

> EBERHARD ARNOLD, from a letter, July 1934

April 7

God himself is the giver. The Spirit gave God's fiery brand into the Son's hand. The torch of wrath became the giver of life. The glowing heat of judgment has gushed forth into the fire of life. It lives in the light of love which liberates and gathers us.

> EBERHARD ARNOLD, *Innenland*,
> "Light and Fire"

April 8

We celebrate Easter, not in memory of a Jesus who once arose from the dead; but in honor of God, because He gives us the life that is greater than death; because in every affliction and every death in our lives the victory can be ours. For our Lord Jesus Christ is the resurrection and the life.

> CHRISTOPH BLUMHARDT, *Blumhardt Calendar*

April 9

Where the life-giving Spirit of the peace of God fills and unites men, it expresses its infinite power in an activity of love which is as many-sided as it is unified, as moved and stirred as it is firm and steadfast, as manifold and varied as it is whole and undivided.

> EBERHARD ARNOLD, *Innenland*,
> "The Peace of God"

April 10

Our inner fire, yes, even our enthusiasm, our inspiration, and soul, and Eros—everything that is fire and love—must flow together with the one great light, with the holy Agape, with the heart of God, with Jesus Christ; and being born out of Him, it must gain new life in purity and power. It is quite clear that this means that everything which is greed, desire for possession, despotism, the demand of the individual, is consumed and completely spent in this sun-fire. The one—the old world with its greed for possession—perishes, and the other—the new creation with its divine life that dedicates, embraces, and pours itself out in joy—is born.

EBERHARD ARNOLD, from a letter, July 1922

April 11

He who believes in the all-commanding might of God is filled with courage and certainty for the victory of His peace. Faith in the peace of God is the courage of the heart that is confident of victory.

EBERHARD ARNOLD, *Innenland*, "The Peace of God"

April 12

O merciful Lord! We want to follow thee, our only light. Help us, so that we may know how to walk with thee and cling to thee. Help us to overcome everything evil that this world brings with it. Be our strong Redeemer who does not cease working for our salvation until everything is carried out according to our need. O Lord, come soon with thy mercies. They will bring the promised redemption to its goal. O Lord, help us and bless us and all who look up to thee today. Amen.

JOHANN CHRISTOPH BLUMHARDT,
Blumhardt Calendar

April 13

Everyone who asks is dear to God; for he stands closer to Him than one who does not ask. God does not fail to consider every prayer that is sincere. It is only that He answers in a different way. Yet how often He does it in such a way that we must marvel and adore!

JOHANN CHRISTOPH BLUMHARDT,
Questions of Faith

More is accomplished by prayer if one carries it quietly on one's heart than if one uses many words about it every day.

Questions of Faith

April 14

The peace of God brings the strength of the life of God. It brings the power of His love. It consists of active service. It lives in deed. To the first call, "Lay down your arms!" belongs the second, "Take up your tools!"

EBERHARD ARNOLD, *Innenland*,
"The Peace of God"

April 15

The mighty spirit of the divine light of heaven appears, like the sun, to all men, as the life-giving and life-sustaining power of universal fire.

In the light and unity of Jesus Christ, God's heart of glowing, flaming love has achieved the fulfilment of His eternal will.

EBERHARD ARNOLD, *Innenland*,
"Light and Fire"

April 16

Jesus went through the baptism of blood

in His crucifixion. Following Him, the Church suffered martyrdom and death. This testifies to surrender in total sacrifice, like that of a burnt offering upon the altar fire.

EBERHARD ARNOLD, *Innenland*,
"Light and Fire"

April 17

No power other than the Holy Spirit of Jesus Christ brings kingly freedom. For only He who is mightier than all other spirits is able to bring the authority and lordship of the Father of Jesus Christ to victory over the enslaving powers of death.

EBERHARD ARNOLD, *Innenland*,
"Light and Fire"

April 18

The task that Jesus sets His Church is something completely different from the violent justice of the world state. This task is to hold up in contrast to the justice of violence, brotherly justice, which is the peace of unity and the joy of love.

EBERHARD ARNOLD, *Innenland*,
"Light and Fire"

April 19

Certainly this relationship, between the divine and the human, lives in all men and especially in all deep and vital men; in a particular way it lives in today's young people. In Jesus, however, this relationship attained such a unique and decisive power that we can understand why early Christianity recognized Him as the highest type of man and at the same time as the highest revelation of God.

> EBERHARD ARNOLD, from a letter, Mar. 1920

April 20

I consider it an error on your part when you say that love is an ethical principle which opposes that which is living in Jesus. I agree with Tolstoy in believing that love, and nothing else, is life.

> EBERHARD ARNOLD, from a letter, Mar. 1920

We have finally renounced either doing anything or falsifying anything. We want life as it is; and the last and deepest essence of life is God.

> EBERHARD ARNOLD, from a letter, June 1920

April 21

I am convinced that the strong and victorious spirit of Christ will show itself among us as the power which joins, the power which overcomes everything. In this spirit I give you my hand and greet you from the crumbling world-city which we must now finally leave.

EBERHARD ARNOLD, from a letter, June 1920

April 22

While everything perishes and escapes like a river, and threatens to drown in the stream, the Almighty stands on the heights. When He speaks a word, feeble man can grasp the Almighty by this word. Then flee, ye years! Perish, thou earth! We no longer belong to you. We hold in our hands the rope by which we swing ourselves up into heaven, whence we heard thy voice.

CHRISTOPH BLUMHARDT, "Behold, I Make All Things New!"

April 23

In your lines I feel a deep lack of Holy Spirit and the warm heart of Jesus. I do not have the impression at all that the social question is solved by conversion; for this a long path of healing is needed, and at the same time intervention by God himself.

> EBERHARD ARNOLD, from a letter, Mar. 1920

April 24

We are filled with the faith that the living Spirit of Christ is today causing countless small focal points to arise, where not only community of gathering and building up is to be found, but real community of life and of productive work and vocation.

> EBERHARD ARNOLD, from a letter, Apr. 1920

April 25

You know very well how things are in general amongst the nations. The murder-weapons are ready. The powers of darkness have risen and want to drive things to the point where the earth becomes a pool of blood. Satan knows quite well that if such a thing came about, it would be the end of the preaching of the Gospel.

> CHRISTOPH BLUMHARDT, "Behold, I Make All Things New!"

April 26

Only the Spirit of Christ can guarantee such a working together. It is a fact that today the Spirit is again urging the realization of this communal life. All are expecting the Christians to give an example; all expect that they will be able to attain what others seek in vain. In our circles, in us all, there is still much weakness. Yet I have the invincible certainty that our small strength will urge us toward results that do not come from ourselves.

EBERHARD ARNOLD, from a letter, Apr. 1920

April 27

We must give up everything, give up what is false. We must become completely true, ... just as the Lord Jesus is whole and true and all the angels are true, and God himself. So you also must become true. This is what "new" means. It is comforting that this new thing is not something unheard of. It is practically at our doorstep. It is already on the earth.

CHRISTOPH BLUMHARDT, "Behold, I Make All Things New!"

April 28

Each one of us, of course, must preserve his inner freedom, so that each one follows the holy Shall and the holy Must that lives within him, without making himself in any way dependent.

> EBERHARD ARNOLD, from a letter, Apr. 1920

April 29

There is a power which drives us into far-away lands, to the strangest peoples. This same power drives us also here at home down into the darkest company, into the most degenerate areas of human life. It is our task to long for the Savior to enter those places. We must, if possible, carry this longing where it is darkest, where hope has almost been given up, where ruin and corruption stare back at us and take away our breath. Shall we lose courage? No! For we know that Jesus Christ says, "I give my life for the world."

> CHRISTOPH BLUMHARDT, "I Am With You!"

April 30

We all look forward very much to the great things that we hope will come to us in Schluechtern, at the Steckelsburg and in the mountains there.

The things you mention in your letter could be answered only in a personal discussion. You know that I am always ready for such a meeting of genuine friendship in mutual honesty and love. I was especially glad about the sentence in which you said you felt that the religious forces of the present are seeking a new expression which goes directly back to Jesus.

EBERHARD ARNOLD, from letters,
May 1920

May 1

I start again anew to live,
The night retreats, Death sinks away.
The body wants to stir again.
The Spring flows in, the sunlight calls.

I start again to have new faith,
New courage rises, the spirit wakes.
I'm striding as through rose-filled arbors,
Life widens spreading over all.

So do I start again to love,
Spring's light and scent now fill the air.
Death's coldness presently is scattered,
The dark and loveless night gone by.

Who grasps the lightning, holds the sun?
The lightning kindles, the sun flames forth.
To be puls'd through with the awesome
 vision
Is blessed waiting to him who sees.

>   EBERHARD ARNOLD, 1923

May 2

In trembling reverence, man stands in wonder before the life-filled tree, by the living bubbling spring, under the life-giving radiant stars of day and night, in the midst of the fruitfulness of earth and its life. How great and mighty must God be, who brings forth and sustains all things! Into a powerfully shaken and moved heart comes the demand: the great Creator God must become undisputed ruler over all this powerful life.

>   EBERHARD ARNOLD, *Innenland*,
>   "The Experience of God"

May 3

God does not work by only one method, paint in only one color, play in only one key, nor does He make only one star shine onto the earth. God's mystery is the rich spectrum of color that is gathered together in the purity of the sun's white light. The symphonic harmony of all the stars is built up on precisely their manifold variety. But all this is gathered together and will be gathered together at the end of time in the unity of the kingdom of God.

EBERHARD ARNOLD, May 1935

May 4

In the Easter message and in the Pentecostal flame of the Holy Spirit, the sacred spring of youth sets out to consecrate new land to the Church of the risen Christ through the holy fire of the eternal Spirit.

EBERHARD ARNOLD, *Innenland*,
"Light and Fire"

May 5

We cling to a divine time which will rule over us and fill our years on earth with His will. We know well that the day of God is not yet achieved; and that which this time is to bring has not yet been fulfilled. But that makes no difference to us. We want to go on living in God's Word every day, firm and hopeful and believing and full of love. For the day of God radiates faith, it radiates hope, it radiates love in Jesus Christ.

> CHRISTOPH BLUMHARDT, *Blumhardt Calendar*

May 6

The peace of God is the living, effective, infinitely rich and moving harmony of life to the full. "Whoso findeth me, findeth life"—that is the revelation it brings.

> EBERHARD ARNOLD, *Innenland*, "The Peace of God"

May 7

The Gospel consists in saying to all men, "God lays his hand upon you, not to crush you but to help you. So accept this help, and you will find that God is your Father."

> CHRISTOPH BLUMHARDT, *Blumhardt Calendar*

May 8

It is the greatest foolishness to think that as Christians we must be like great heroes. God always works through weak men. Yet they are the strongest, because in them the hope for the Spirit's power can work most purely.

The great thing about the ascension of the Lord Jesus Christ is that He remains and we have Him, although He rises up to heaven. Let us rejoice! The Lord will yet do great things and we shall marvel at His glory and mercy!

CHRISTOPH BLUMHARDT, *Blumhardt Calendar*

May 9

The believing and loving people who are united in the holy flame protect not themselves but the flame of the Spirit which is the only assurance of true life. They do not seek to keep their own life; they seek alone that of the holy fire in which they have lost their own nature.

EBERHARD ARNOLD, *Innenland*, "Light and Fire"

May 10

Either you become new, or you perish, and you might as well join in the stream of death together with the whole world. But as a Christian, as a disciple of Jesus, one should be horrified to have to swim along in this stream of death. Defend yourselves, then!

> CHRISTOPH BLUMHARDT, "Behold, I Make All Things New!"

May 11

That great new thing which is germinating and sprouting everywhere has not yet taken shape. We know that a strong religious wave is in the process of growing. We know that it is the Spirit of Christ which storms over us as a new, fresh wind, though we cannot or will not say whence it comes or whither it goes. It is the Spirit of the same Jesus who brought into reality a life and death of complete and unconditional love. It is the all-embracing Spirit of the Logos of Christ through which all things which exist came into being.

> EBERHARD ARNOLD, invitation to Whitsun Conference, 1920

May 12

We all have the impression more and more that it is not much help to us to go into an abstract analysis of how this Spirit works and takes shape. But we do need one another, we who are under the freeing and liberating influences of this Spirit. We want to know one another and experience together what the life-giving Spirit does amongst us.

EBERHARD ARNOLD, invitation to Whitsun Conference, 1920

May 13

From the hour when you learned to know the Savior, He penetrates with His meekness and humility, with His life and death into all your days, down into the first day of your life. Backwards into all your days the redeeming spirit of Jesus pierces, backwards where so much in you was wrong. Thus you may be comforted even in your past. Thus you may say about your past, "Even then God was with me."

CHRISTOPH BLUMHARDT, "I Am With You!"

May 14

Multitudes will soon be singing
From the lofty halls and vast,
With strange sounds the air a-ringing
And the mighty organ blast;
Sounds that set the echoes ringing
When mankind repents at last.

Come, thou day when from the shadows
Shall arise a new mankind;
Morning of a thousand rainbows,
Men at one in heart and mind;
When the rushing, mighty wind blows,
Whitsuntide of all mankind.

> HANS FIEHLER, known as "HANS IM GLUECK", 1924

May 15

All the birch trees grow green now on heath and moor,
Every gorse bush is shining gold;
All the skylarks are piping a song of joy,
Moorhens whirring in gladness untold.

And my eyes are wandering here and there
O'er the dark of the white-flecked moor,
O'er the brown heather sea, with its foaming green,
'Til they rise up to heaven's door.

A quiet song, a peaceful song,
A song so tender and fine,
Like a cloudlet that over the blue sky sails,
Like cotton-grass blown in the wind.

> HERMANN LOENS, from the youth movement in Germany

May 16

The world must die in order to be born again. But as long as the salt in the world remains salt it opposes evil, acting as the power which one day will renew the earth and all mankind.

> EBERHARD ARNOLD, "Studies in the Sermon on the Mount"

May 17

How great are God and His kingdom! How great is the historical hour of world crisis, world distress and world catastrophe; how much greater still is God's hour of judgment of the world and Christ's hour of liberation that is coming! How burning our desire should be to know all these things more and more deeply and to share in them; how fervently we should expect and long for the day itself, the coming day, that will bring freedom and unity!

> EBERHARD ARNOLD, from a letter, Nov. 1935

May 18

The abyss between the two mortally opposed armies is the abyss between the present and the future, between the existent era and the coming epoch of history. Therefore the heroism of Jesus is at variance with the spirit of the age in every respect. But the character of His way is to subject all present conditions and relationships of life to the coming purpose of the future.

> EBERHARD ARNOLD, *The Early Christians*

May 19

The assumption that one's prayer is not answered is not always justified. Basically it is never justified, even if everything is in order on the part of the one praying. For the fact that an answer is not immediately seen is not yet proof that God does not answer. It may possibly take a long time before fruit of an intercession is seen. Yet the Lord is already working in secret toward it.

> Johann Christoph Blumhardt, *Questions of Faith*

May 20

Let us be joyful together. Then we shall be as a house into which the Lord Jesus will gladly enter ... A new time will begin once the Lord Jesus has truly made His dwelling on earth. We must step back and become His servants. Then whatever we do will bear the stamp of His work.

> Christoph Blumhardt, "I Am With You!"

May 21

There are many who uphold a hope for the future. Their thinking is Christian. Yet they have trouble keeping the adversary out of their hearts. With arts and sciences, with all our human thinking, the adversary wants to rob us of the little flame in our hearts. I beg you, my friends, do not believe in such things! Be quite certain that everything we men need has been revealed in Jesus Christ, in His words and deeds.

> CHRISTOPH BLUMHARDT, "Our Human Right"

May 22

The love to Jesus, this burning personal love to God who has made himself known to us, is and remains the witness to the unity of all-embracing life. This love as the deepest and most heartfelt personal relationship finds its living expression in calling upon the One it loves. The truth and force of this love, however, lies in the decisive fact that it is God, really God, whom it meets in Christ. One who really believes in God as He is and works, will be urged again and again to communicate with Him.

> EBERHARD ARNOLD, "The Meaning and Power of Prayer Life"

May 23

We are living in the old reality, which completely occupies all our senses. It is the old story of perishing, of wasting away, and behind it lies a mighty darkness: death ... In Jesus a new reality appears, a reality which is opposed to the reality of world history ... This new history must become revealed in each individual person: in you, in me, in all of us.

CHRISTOPH BLUMHARDT, "The New Reality"

May 24

Keep your courage and hold fast to the holy expectation! The faith and the love of Jesus Christ will give you the great thoughts which are worthy of this great hour. The more evil the hour, the greater it becomes for the Gospel and for the task of the Church. Do not be alarmed! God is greater than our hearts. The believing heart can embrace greater things than the whole world can imagine. Surrender every single thing into the whole! Let the great things rule over all small things!

EBERHARD ARNOLD, from a letter, May 1935

May 25

They that toward springs of righteousness are thronging
From God's full hand shall yet receive their longing;

And the pure-hearted, as it hath been told
  them,
They shall behold Him.

His loving-kindness frees us from our
  fearing,
All our proud boasting dies at His
  appearing.
All our self-seeking serves but to undo us;
God must renew us!
    OTTO SALOMON, Sannerz, 1921

May 26

The valley opens wide,
Warm sunshine floods the earth with light;
Oh, may my heart awake to Thee,
Be opened, opened wide!
That I for Thee may be outpoured,
In stillness now may wait for Thee!

No other choice is mine;
Eternity rules in the spheres.
Eternally light's rays stream forth,
Not in one place to shine,
But everywhere! Space is for Thee!
I give myself, I trust, believe.

God, Thou art great, so great.
To Thee the widest land is small;
Thy Spirit is unbounded, free.

We love Thee without end;
Surrendered wholly to Thy call,
I lose myself, to live in Thee!

    EBERHARD ARNOLD, Sannerz

May 27

The fullness of God cannot endure any private life of self, however pious. He who toils to keep himself and his salvation and inner life afloat is still occupied with himself and has no strength for loving. But he who has been saved from the death-bringing, isolated life of self takes part in the all-embracing life power of God's unity, and will give this power to his deliverer as love which goes out to all. In this unity, then, all who will accept the Word in Jesus will be set free.

    EBERHARD ARNOLD, "The Meaning and Power of Prayer Life"

May 28

God is life. He is so abounding in life that His nature is love. The life of God is the will for unity and community. The heart of His righteousness is the gathering love which draws together and unites, and makes everything communal which belongs to life. Where life is stronger than death, it is revealed as love.

> EBERHARD ARNOLD, "Love to the Brothers"

May 29

Christ has given us a new commandment —to love one another as He has loved us. This love renews and makes us new men, singers of the new song. This love renews the peoples. Out of the whole of mankind which is spread over the entire globe, this love creates and gathers the new people, the body of the new spouse, the bride of the only Son of God. About her the Song of Songs sings: "Who is it who rises up in a white garment? Why does she walk in a white garment, unless it is because she is made new?"

> AUGUSTINE

May 30

The Pentecostal spring of the early Christian Church stands in the strongest contrast to the icily rigid Christianity of our day. Everyone feels that there a fresher wind blows and purer water springs, that there a stronger power and a more glowing warmth hold sway than is the case today among those who call themselves Christians.

>   EBERHARD ARNOLD, *Innenland*,
>   "The Holy Spirit"

May 31

There is absolutely no obstacle that can prevail against the Holy Spirit; space, time, death—all come to an end. At Pentecost the Spirit is there. Therefore the Christian Church is so firmly founded that nothing earthly can ever demolish it, because the Holy Spirit once came to the earth. And just as the Lord Jesus will not let himself be parted from us, neither will the Holy Spirit be parted from us.

>   CHRISTOPH BLUMHARDT, *Blumhardt Calendar*

June 1

The City-Church of God lives only in the pure air of its eternal hill.

>   EBERHARD ARNOLD, *Innenland*,
>   "The Holy Spirit"

June 2

Jesus has kindled in mankind the rulership of His peace from the other world.

EBERHARD ARNOLD, *Innenland*,
"The Peace of God"

June 3

In the Church, the beginning of the coming kingdom is present in its full power and challenging clarity.

EBERHARD ARNOLD, *Innenland*,
"The Peace of God"

June 4

The message of the Gospel is the awakening from death. From the resurrection on, Christ is proving himself the Son of God in the constantly renewed coming down of the Holy Spirit.

EBERHARD ARNOLD, *Innenland*

June 5

Life and life-community must rise towards the sun like the sun-bird phoenix, always being burned to ashes, yet being renewed again and again.

EBERHARD ARNOLD, *Innenland*

June 6

Where Jesus' influence makes men into real men, their life becomes genuine and pure. It shines into the darkness of the world around and unmasks what is false and untrue—what is trying to hide. But the light which Jesus kindles is not exhausted by just making a situation clear. Cold light has no part in the kingdom of God. What matters is to live in God's heart and from God's heart. As with the sun, the brightness of His being is inseparable from life-kindling warmth.

EBERHARD ARNOLD, "Studies in the Sermon on the Mount"

June 7

With light and power all are set on fire for the work of love.

EBERHARD ARNOLD, *Innenland*, "The Holy Spirit"

June 8

In God, as the central sun of our being, we find the middle point of our inner life, because we recognize in Him the central fire of all creation and of all history and of the history of the end of all things.

> EBERHARD ARNOLD, *Innenland*, "The Inner Life"

June 9

I have faith that in these days of political world crisis the hour has come near when many will turn away from world politics and will seek a better way of justice, national community and peace among men, turning towards that government which knows no other kingdom than the one that is truly of God.

> EBERHARD ARNOLD, from a letter, June 1934

June 10

When the soul is set on fire by the Holy Spirit it triumphs in the body; a great fire of new life arises in it.

> EBERHARD ARNOLD, *Innenland*, "Light and Fire"

June 11

We have, each in a different way, a gift and a service to perform for the body of the Church; and we need the services and gifts of others, as they need ours.

We must go forward. The word of the Spirit must become ever more clear and sharp, the expression of love more pure and tender.

EBERHARD ARNOLD, from a letter, Nov. 1919

June 12

The peace of God is the unity and wholeness of His creative spirit, which wants to bring the torn state of man and of the whole world into God's unity of peace which must be built up anew.

Self in man is what hinders the unity of God. When men do good, the peace of God takes the place of divisive evil.

EBERHARD ARNOLD, *Innenland*, "The Peace of God"

June 13

The Lord of peace wholly consecrates and sanctifies men and human life to His perfect purity and unity. He demands the surrender of life and everything belonging to it.

Peace belongs to all those who do good, who surrender everything to love, and it belongs to them alone. Peace streams from the mercy of God. It reveals His heart.

> EBERHARD ARNOLD, *Innenland*,
> "The Peace of God"

June 14

Even at a distance the Lord is able to arouse participation in those who belong to Him. He gives them an opportunity to render help to their friends through intercession. For God's will often requires intercession, so that there may be two who pray.

> JOHANN CHRISTOPH BLUMHARDT,
> *Questions of Faith*

June 15

When we experience a truth through the Holy Spirit, then we are free from the world. Then we can also endure world history. We can think: The Holy Spirit is coming and will yet rule world history, so that men will awaken to God and to Jesus Christ. Then we will not only ask, "Lord Jesus, come!" Even more earnestly we will ask, "Lord Jesus, speak for us before God the Father's throne when we ask: Send us the Holy Spirit! Send us the Spirit of truth, the Comforter, the Teacher! We need Him even more than thy disciples who saw thee!"

  CHRISTOPH BLUMHARDT, *Blumhardt Calendar*

June 16

The only thing required is that we continue in unconditional truthfulness and in complete love, and that we see the help and the solution in nothing but Jesus alone.

  EBERHARD ARNOLD, from a letter, Feb. 1920

I can only say that I feel more and more certain and more and more happy in my inner calling to deeds in the love of Jesus, and to the discipleship of Christ in all aspects of practical life.

  EBERHARD ARNOLD, from a letter, Mar. 1920

June 17

When you look back over your life you may recall many days of which you are ashamed. Yet you must believe! If you are even now moved by God's Spirit and repent, then surely Jesus was also present in the days when you did not know Him yet.

> CHRISTOPH BLUMHARDT, "I Am With You!"

June 18

We feel very much that we need a time of quiet and of intensive common work before we can begin on any bigger new undertakings. Because of this we believe that for now the right way is being given to us in a small communal settlement; this will be in the neighborhood of Schluechtern. But it would be very important to us to be able to have a close contact with you all from there.

> EBERHARD ARNOLD, from a letter, June 1920

June 19

Many think that God can be proclaimed only through what is good. No! No, indeed! Unless we ourselves are again and again saved from fear and suffering, we are nothing to the world. We Christians are no good at all unless we are born anew from God, brought back to life from death. Unless we go through suffering and sorrow because Jesus is with us, unless in Him we can overcome all afflictions however deep they may be, we shall be no good in the world.

    CHRISTOPH BLUMHARDT, "I Am With You!"

June 20

The Word, anew revealed,
Shines out with truth and light.
We view in deepest wonder
The Spirit's new-built house.

To truth awakened newly
We wait to hear God's call,
And step by step He leads us
The way He longs for all.

His way is newly opened;
His Kingdom comes so near.
His message is all-powerful,
Our Strengthener is here.

    EBERHARD ARNOLD, 1921

June 21

The eye is created for the light. In the same measure that the life born of light gains ground, the eye becomes able to bear light.

EBERHARD ARNOLD, *Innenland*,
"Light and Fire"

June 22

The center of this new people is the new fire of the new Church; once more there arises around it the dwelling-place of its community. Around the radiant fire of the Holy Spirit its spiritual temple is built up as a tangible house of God. It is the City on the Hill, whose light shines into all lands. Its place of worship burns in spirit; it shines in truth.

EBERHARD ARNOLD, *Innenland*,
"Light and Fire"

June 23

Everything that we men need has been revealed in Jesus Christ, in His words and deeds. Where else are we to turn, to overcome sin, if not to this judging forgiveness which came to us in Jesus Christ? How else can we fight against evil, if not with this clarity of the living power which shall one day illumine even our bodies? How are we to come unscathed through all the chaos among men unless the peace revealed through Jesus Christ enters into our hearts, this peace which Jesus proclaimed even in the presence of His enemies? How can we stand above the human turmoil and conflict unless our hearts are moved by the divine purpose?

    CHRISTOPH BLUMHARDT, "Our Human Right"

June 24

Soul, strength and courage kindling,
Come, fire that quickeneth.
Let us through thy pure burning
Condemn the works of death.
Burn clear, and bright sparks flying,
The love of God streams glowing forth,
All darkness overcoming.

O holy fire, make flaming
Our hearts now cold and dead.
O timid lips, proclaim Him
Who helps in every need.
The inward light now leads us;
Light-sanctified, draw close the ring,
Be ready for His service.

    TRUDI HUESSY, 1928

June 25

Anyone who suffers from a lack of love must seek the renewing of his life in the deepest faith of the Church and in the power of the Holy Spirit. Only then will he be able to remain firm in the love of God. For his whole life will be turned in holy expectation toward the heart of Jesus and His coming eternity.

> Eberhard Arnold, "Love to the Brothers"

June 26

Because the believer has himself recognized, in the word of truth and in the life and deeds and death of Jesus, that holiness in which the love of God is dwelling, he is constantly aware of what separates and divides men from this unity which is the only source of life. He must thank God anew for the certainty that his sin is taken away and forgiven by God himself. He is one with God and His Church through the victory of Jesus over the evil deeds of the demonic powers of self. He goes to meet God in complete confidence.

> Eberhard Arnold, "The Meaning and Power of Prayer Life"

June 27

Let's walk in the open country,
Over the meadows far,
Out where the lonely summits
Clear in their beauty are;
Listening whence blow the storm-winds chill,
Looking what lands lie beyond the hill,
Earth stretching wide and far.

And deep in the wood there is blooming
The tiny flower blue;
And just to win this flower
We'll travel the wide world through.
The trees are a-rustle, the stream murmurs slow,
And he who to seek the flower blue would go
Must be a wanderer too!

> Wandervogel text and tune

June 28

The age of God lies in the future; but it has already been revealed. Its nature and its power have become personal and historical in Jesus. They have been shown forth in His words. They have fought through to victory in His life work.

EBERHARD ARNOLD, *The Early Christians*

June 29

The new future brings to an end all existing ruling powers, all systems of law and property. The coming kingdom of God is already revealed as unity in the perfect love of God, and therefore as devoted brotherhood of men. Jesus proclaimed and brought God alone, God's coming rule and empire alone. Jesus founded neither churches nor sects.

EBERHARD ARNOLD, *The Early Christians*

June 30

He who was put to an ignominious death is and remains the coming Lord of God's future age. He who was dead has become alive again. The present age is facing its end. The greatest turning point which can occur in the history of the world and in the order of creation is imminent. Jesus will come for the second time with authority and glory. Then the rule of God shall be established over the whole earth.

> EBERHARD ARNOLD, *The Early Christians*

July 1

Ever again a longing rises,
Again we look toward a time
When into darkness, gloom and trouble
Eternity's bright light will shine.

Ever again dark clouds o'ershadow
The radiant light of a new day;
Cold, creeping mists hide from our vision
Paths we have known, and hope's new way.

Again the first new love is living,
The first belief, steadfast and true.
O man, awake, and give thy powers
To Jesus Christ, thy Lord, anew!

> FRITZ KLEINER, 1944

July 2

If we ask God earnestly that His will may become a fact on earth, that His nature may be revealed in work, that His rulership may lead men to unity, righteousness and love, then our life will become work. Faith without works is dead. Prayer without work is hypocrisy. The Lord's Prayer without the way of God's kingdom is a lie. The prayer of Jesus wants to bring us to the point where its words are turned into deeds, so that the prayer becomes action and history.

> EBERHARD ARNOLD, "The Meaning and Power of Prayer Life"

July 3

The Word of God was living before the first pages of the Bible were written. It was living at the beginning of all things.

> EBERHARD ARNOLD, *Innenland*, "The Living Word"

July 4

He who wants to be born of God must be mindful of how Christ's birth took place.

> EBERHARD ARNOLD, *Innenland*, "The Living Word"

July 5

We are able to cope with the demands of today's need only when we have found the inward concentration in God. And this we find only when the lightning of God's kingdom has fallen down to earth and lit up the whole horizon.

> EBERHARD ARNOLD, *Innenland*,
> "The Inner Life"

July 6

Where God heals and makes well, He grants perfect peace on the basis of faithfulness and of faith. He who follows the Spirit says with the prophet, "As long as I live, peace and faithfulness shall reign."

> EBERHARD ARNOLD, *Innenland*,
> "The Peace of God"

July 7

The present time with all its pain and sin and corruption is to have an end. The Lord Jesus will be with us until the end of this world of death, this world of sin, this world of folly. He will be with us until the end of this world which causes so much heartache.

CHRISTOPH BLUMHARDT, "I Am With You!"

July 8

How glad I am that you are so positively united with me in the experience of peace and of Jesus' spirit of love! The question is not at all one of our only refusing to do military service, though people always put it in this negative way. This refusal, after all, follows as a matter of course from a positive experience of the Spirit of Christ. When this Spirit, which is expressed so very intensely in the Sermon on the Mount and in Romans 8, penetrates us and glows in us, then we will become victorious people who must work as long as it is daylight—work in the productive, creative work of love.

EBERHARD ARNOLD, from a letter, May 1920

July 9

Let us always work together, upright and clear and at the same time in faith and confident joy. Christ gives us this possibility of putting truth into practice as love, and love as purity and freedom.

> EBERHARD ARNOLD, from a letter, June 1920

July 10

Outside of Jesus' person there is nothing to kindle a light in our hearts, nothing to support our hope for the future of mankind. When the image of Jesus Christ departs from our hearts, when the truly living and abiding presence of the Lord Jesus is lost, the light of hope is extinguished. We can have no hope for the world without the person of Jesus Christ.

> CHRISTOPH BLUMHARDT, "Our Human Right"

July 11

Where can we find the meaning
For all earth's need and care?
We must be truly humble
For God to draw us near.
First must be born within us
A pure and simple child;
Then we have joy beholding
God's likeness undefiled.

Joy is the fount of being
That springs throughout all life;
We must ourselves surrender
If even unto death.
There is but one forgiveness,
That is when God forgives.
There is but one true source of life,
When God gives us His love.

OTTO SALOMON, 1921

July 12

It was Jesus who showed and brought and gave us God's nature and power. Ever since He came, it is possible for us to pray to the Father in spirit and in truth. This spirit of truth makes us free from the impure mixing of religious practices with their human emphasis on what is outward and their idolatrous materialization. It brings us into the unified realm of the pure Church of God and of God's unconditional rulership. This truth is the essence and reality of God's genuine, clear word as it has gone forth from Him from the beginning.

EBERHARD ARNOLD, "The Meaning and Power of Prayer Life"

July 13

Our all-inclusive task is to awaken the people of Israel to the impending catastrophe, to shake out of sleep the whole of mankind before their certain overthrow, that all may be prepared for the coming Kingdom.

EBERHARD ARNOLD, *The Early Christians*

July 14

Oneness with the triumphant Christ makes the tragic conflict with the dark powers of this world epoch into a soldier's life, which is certain of victory against the greatest enemy of all time. No bloody weapons, no amulets, no magic formulas or ceremonies are to be employed in this war.

EBERHARD ARNOLD, *The Early Christians*

July 15

God stands above every event. Faith can withstand the storm of all forces only if we are one with God. It is not men who stand firm. God alone is invincible. In Him alone is the freedom of soul that guards against bondage to even the strongest force.

Eberhard Arnold, *Innenland*,
"The Experience of God"

July 16

God has come near. Man can be in God. God wants to be known and experienced. But we tremble at this. The experience of God is terrifying, for it brings the discovery of truth. We fear the light of God, because it makes our darkness known.

Eberhard Arnold, *Innenland*,
"The Experience of God"

July 17

God himself was the only one who was able to restore himself and His lost image to us. He did this in Jesus Christ. In Jesus, God's heart came into our midst anew. In Him it became clear again what God's will and Spirit is.

Eberhard Arnold, *Innenland*,
"The Experience of God"

July 18

The tremendous thing in Jesus Christ is that this unity is reached by unveiling the truth. Its light comes to us in all its sharpness. When men experience God in Jesus Christ, they experience His being as holiness which judges their sin and yet draws them into His unity.

> EBERHARD ARNOLD, *Innenland*,
> "The Experience of God"

July 19

God bursts open our present nature with all our life and action as it has been until now. He wants to bring forth from the ruins the original and ultimate humanity.
Our own work must stop, so that His work may begin. It must begin in us. It must be established through us.

> EBERHARD ARNOLD, *Innenland*,
> "The Experience of God"

July 20

The experience of God unites and separates at the same time. The deeper His love leads into community with His heart and into brotherly uniting of men, the more seriously we become aware of the absolute difference between our sin, which is separation, and His purity, which is unity. Between men and God there is the sharpest contrast. God wants unity, but without concealing what is in opposition.

> EBERHARD ARNOLD, *Innenland*,
> "The Experience of God"

July 21

It is always a matter of the clashing of two opposing goals. One goal seeks the person of high position, the great person, the spiritual person, the clever person, the fine person, who because of his natural abilities exhibits a special talent in the high places of mankind. And the other goal seeks the lowly people, the suffering people, who because of their low position live in a valley; who in the high places of mankind create the low place; the humble people, those who are wrongfully enslaved, the exploited and the weak and poor, the poorest of the poor.

> EBERHARD ARNOLD, spoken in a meeting, Oct. 1934

July 22

Jesus experienced the utmost humiliation, which led Him very much lower than He had been at His birth in the feed-trough, in the manger. When Jesus was hung on the cross and crucified, the high official, that proud representative of the whole Roman Empire, said, shortly before this overpowering humiliation, "Behold, a man." Behold the man! Jesus, the man! He who reveals God as a man, this is the one whom we seek. He who reveals God as love, this is the human being with whom we want to have communion.

> Eberhard Arnold, spoken in a
> meeting, Oct. 1934

July 23

The love of God is poured into our hearts through the Holy Spirit. This is what really becoming human means. Besides, out of this love that which God wants must be created: our truly becoming human; the embodiment of the eternal Christ in complete love, in complete community, in complete peace, in complete unity! I am always so thankful when we are together with guests and friends and they, by their contrasting points of view, remind us that we may return anew to that which alone is decisive, to the way of Jesus Christ, who was humiliated.

> Eberhard Arnold, spoken in a meeting, Oct. 1934

July 24

We want to ask for all men that they may be released from the delusion of self-exaltation and of becoming "wonderful" people. We want to ask that they may understand the meaning of history and the significance of the human being in relation to Jesus Christ who is the complete human being. He is the new human being toward whom we may grow because of our belonging to Him. So that out of Him, through Him and in Him, men will become new. This change will begin in the body of Christ, which is the Church.

> Eberhard Arnold, spoken in a meeting, Oct. 1934

July 25

I am the Lord who gives strength in the day of tribulation. Come to me when it is not well with you. This is what most hinders you, that you are too slow to turn yourself to me. For before you earnestly ask me, you seek many comforts, and look for refreshment in outward things. And thus it comes to pass that everything profits you little, until you consider well that I am He who rescues them that trust in Him and that, besides me, there is neither powerful help, nor profitable counsel, nor lasting remedy. Now take heart and trust in me, gather strength in the light of mercies; for I am at hand to help you.

THOMAS A KEMPIS, *Imitation of Christ*

July 26

The small world of the individual man must reflect the great world of God's history. To experience God means to surrender to the goal of His kingdom so that one accepts His judgment of death and believes in His resurrection. The power of the future comes to the believer. Through the active Spirit of the coming Christ he receives already in the present the calling to live for the future.

EBERHARD ARNOLD, *Innenland*, "The Experience of God"

July 27

Be not conformed to this world; but be

ye transformed by the renewing of your mind, that ye may prove what is that good, and acceptable, and perfect, will of God.

Letter to the Romans 12, 2
(Authorized Version)

Don't let the world around you squeeze you into its own mold, but let God remold your minds from within, so that you may prove in practice that the plan of God for you is good, meets all His demands and moves toward the goal of true maturity.

Letter to the Romans 12, 2
(J. B. Phillips translation)

July 28

To the prophetic view, God appears as the guide and shepherd of all history. He guides men's external destinies towards the one goal, which is the uniting of all nations in one fold.

Man is received into the domain of God's kingdom. The essence of this kingdom is the rulership of love.

EBERHARD ARNOLD, *Innenland*,
"The Experience of God"

July 29

When the vials of wrath are poured out

over the world, when the need becomes unbearably intense, then a justice must be proclaimed and lived which is stronger than all the injustice of the world and which at the same time fulfils in love the punishing justice of judgment.

EBERHARD ARNOLD, *Innenland*,
"The Experience of God"

July 30

Every experience of God is an undeserved gift. Through the unreserved disclosure of our incapacity and our antagonism to God, we have allowed ourselves to be recognized by God. In the utterly undeserved love of His Son's sacrifice we have recognized Him. We have experienced Jesus as the healing Savior of a life that was going completely to ruin. Through His death we have experienced forgiveness and redemption from the heaviest burden. Each renewed experience of God leads us more and more deeply to the awareness of the deathly bondage of all men in guilt and to thanksgiving for unmerited grace.

EBERHARD ARNOLD, *Innenland*,
"The Experience of God"

July 31

With the Crucified we undergo a death that liberates us from everything which makes community with God impossible. When we are surrendered to the judgment of Jesus' death we become one with the heart of God in a new life. God breaks in. The new life begins. Evil comes to an end. Good begins.

The light of Jesus Christ is the new life of perfect unity. Everything that is without community and opposed to community is darkness and coldness; it is turned away from the glowing light of Jesus.

EBERHARD ARNOLD, *Innenland*,
"The Experience of God"

August 1

Nothing but a last, deepest inward revival, a great, full awakening to God and to His all-determining rule, will be instrumental in carrying into the whole world the Gospel, the glad message of Christ and His unique importance.

EBERHARD ARNOLD, *Innenland*,
Introduction

August 2

There is only one sense in which a man can be a Christian. This is the inner sense, which for this very reason works at the same time upon all that is external. One can be a Christian only when he has experienced within his own heart the decisive word about Christ's nearness.

EBERHARD ARNOLD, *Innenland*,
"The Inner Life"

August 3

Only when the order of unity and clarity is achieved in our innermost being can our life—the unity and freedom of the City on the Hill—attain the warming and radiating power of the light on the lampstand, making it a light for the whole world.

EBERHARD ARNOLD, *Innenland*,
Introduction

August 4

Take courage! We must no longer see what is small! The great must take hold of us in such a way that it also penetrates and transforms the small. I have courage and joy for our life again in the certainty, of course, that it will cost a great and glorious struggle. The Spirit will conquer the flesh! The Spirit is the stronger! He overwhelms me, you, one after the other. This Spirit is goodness, independence, mobility.

EBERHARD ARNOLD, from a letter, July 1922

August 5

Whenever things were really hard and bitter, we always said, "Praise the Lord, O my soul!" Never has anything been overcome by complaining. Never has anything been gained by real vexation and anger, but only by the thought that everything comes to us from God.

CHRISTOPH BLUMHARDT, *Blumhardt Calendar*

August 6

"Behold, I make all things new!" ... We enter into this comfort only through repentance. Many people do not consider sufficiently all that must become new. They think of all sorts of things around them and often not at all of themselves. And if they do think of themselves, they would like to have only certain things changed so that they may go forward again more comfortably. They never consider that all things must become new, everything within you, around you, everything in the whole world.

CHRISTOPH BLUMHARDT, "Behold, I Make All Things New!"

August 7

Recently we buried our father von Hollander. He was a man of soaring spirit and undaunted idealism. He would rather have remained at home in the other world than make compromises in this world which would have destroyed his own nature. At his grave we felt we must remain true to this better kingdom of the true Spirit and of real justice. As citizens of the future kingdom of God, we want already now to grasp and experience its character and its nature.

EBERHARD ARNOLD, from a letter, May 1920

August 8

It is not true, as some think, that mankind will automatically develop to a state of perfection, that our earthly conditions can produce anything good. It is not true that our hearts can find a way out of the confusion, out of our sin, out of our darkness and wrongdoing. It would be false to imagine that we can achieve anything real and true without a faith in Jesus Christ.

CHRISTOPH BLUMHARDT, "Our Human Right"

August 9

The Spirit of the Church has taken care that the revelation of the great times of God has come into our hands: the living words spoken by God through the apostles and prophets, the writings of the living people of God and of the ever-living martyr Church of Jesus.

EBERHARD ARNOLD, "The Meaning and Power of Prayer Life"

August 10

We gather for the holy fight,
We gather in God's power;
The Lord for battle us prepares,
Flame of His Spirit giving.
God's Spirit roused in heart and soul,
What drives us on to victory's goal.
Praise Him! O Alleluia, Alleluia!

And God has filled our heart and soul
With victory's exultation,
We snatch the prey from bitter foe
In holy joy delighting.
We stand in battle until death,
Remaining steadfast in all need.
Praise Him! O Alleluia, Alleluia!

EBERHARD ARNOLD, 1905

August 11

The message of the first disciples of Jesus was the resurrection of the Messiah-Jesus and the kingdom of God which breaks into the world at His second coming. The Prince of death has learned, too late for himself, that the resurrection of Jesus from the dead has decisively broken the power of death.

EBERHARD ARNOLD, *The Early Christians*

August 12

The fact of facts is this, that Christ's whole victory and power is perfected in His suffering and dying and rising again, in His ascension to the throne and in His future second coming. For what Christ has done, He does ever again in His Church. His victory is perfect.

> EBERHARD ARNOLD, *The Early Christians*

August 13

Union with God is possible only when all powers opposed to God, all facts and actions opposed to Him, are radically destroyed. Therefore forgiveness and removal of sin, release and liberation must be the basic substance of every experience of God. Forgiveness is the removal of things as they are. What is hostile to God cannot be present when God unites. He wants perfect purity in uniting. Thus everything that is opposed to purity must be taken away. This is forgiveness. Without this, God's kingdom will not come.

> EBERHARD ARNOLD, *Innenland*, "The Experience of God"

August 14

The lightning descends and reveals the tension between the small "I" of man and the great "Thou" of God. The heart of man, as an "I" that remains very small, worships in complete surrender of will the great "Thou" that gives itself to him in incomprehensible goodness.

EBERHARD ARNOLD, *Innenland*, "The Experience of God"

August 15

Think not yourself wholly left, although for a time you are troubled and have not your desired comfort; for this is the way to the kingdom of heaven. And without doubt, it is better for you and for the rest of the servants, that you sometimes have misfortune than that you should have all things according to your desires. I know the secret thoughts of your heart, and it is for your welfare that you are left sometimes without comfort, lest perhaps you should be puffed up with pride, and think yourself better than you are. What I have given, I can take away; and can restore it again when I please.

THOMAS A KEMPIS, *Imitation of Christ*

August 16

There is no other life of faith than that of the unity and community in which Christ lives. Faith lives in Christ. The deepest relationship of unity is the necessary condition for the restoration and renewal of life. The believer is in Christ and Christ is in him; this is the power that transforms from within all relationships of life.

> EBERHARD ARNOLD, *Innenland*,
> "The Experience of God"

August 17

Only if we accept the whole Christ, for the whole of life, can everything be changed and renewed. It is a lie and a delusion to think that Jesus can be accepted in part, for only part of life. The spirit of life tolerates no choosing of guiding principles or elements of faith, no selecting from God's truth, by a self-willed spirit. Truth is indivisible.

> EBERHARD ARNOLD, *Innenland*,
> "The Experience of God"

August 18

Jesus Christ never draws near in the course of a fleeting, passing impression. Either He brings God's whole kingdom forever, or He gives nothing. Only those who want to receive Him completely and forever can experience Him. To Him it is given to know the secret of God's kingdom.

Wherever there is life that comes from God, life takes on that form which corresponds to the complete image of Jesus Christ, and therefore to the kingdom of God.

EBERHARD ARNOLD, *Innenland,*
"The Experience of God"

August 19

The Christian was baptized into Christ, the Crucified, in such a way that the water of baptism could be compared with the blood of Christ; he had made his own the conflict and victory of the cross against all the demonic powers of the world epoch, and lived from now on in the power and future of the Risen One. He who had broken with all things as they are, had to live and die for the cause to which he had pledged himself in this dedication unto death. With a company of warriors faithful unto death the message broke in upon the old world.

EBERHARD ARNOLD, *The Early Christians*

August 20

We never shall regret that
On rock we've sought to build;
And without fear we're trusting
Alone in God's great love.
He does not hide His goodness,
It breaks into our night;
We know that He will help us
Through grace and by His might.

OTTO SALOMON, Sannerz, 1921

August 21

If the word "faith" has any meaning, it is the certainty of what God—really God, not man—is and does. Faith belongs to God. It does not originate in man. It is God who gives faith and brings it about. The oneness of man with God consists in the faith that comes from God.

Where community is given through faith, this community sets to work at a living activity which is God's doing. In faith, God's power is revealed through human helplessness, God's greatness through human smallness.

EBERHARD ARNOLD, *Innenland*,
"The Experience of God"

August 22

All spirits of human privilege and social injustice are repelled and driven out by the Holy Spirit.

When we pray that God's kingdom may come, we ought to pause and ask ourselves whether we are ready, whether we are willing to accept and to stand up for all the changes that God's rulership brings with it.

> Eberhard Arnold, *Innenland*,
> "The Experience of God"

August 23

The peace of God, as the future of the kingdom of God, must penetrate and hold complete sway over world conditions.

He who believes in the all-commanding might of God is filled with courage and certainty for the victory of His peace. Faith in the peace of God is the courage of the heart that is confident of victory.

> Eberhard Arnold, *Innenland*,
> "The Peace of God"

August 24

Lasting peace can be brought about only by Him who is immortal and eternal. It can never be established by earthly powers. Only the infinite power of God can build up unity and keep peace. All that is mortal is subject to disintegration and dissolution. If unity of life is to be won and kept, death must be overpowered by life.

> EBERHARD ARNOLD, *Innenland*,
> "The Peace of God"

August 25

In the midst of the increasing violence of injustice, in the midst of the widespread coldness of heart and brutality of our time, love shall be revealed. This love towers higher than all earth's mountains and shines out more purely and brightly than all heaven's stars. It is more mighty and powerful than earthquakes and volcanic eruptions, greater than all powers and ruling forces of the world. It has a stronger influence on history than all catastrophes, wars and revolutions, and it is more alive than all the life in creation and its most energetic forces. Above all nature and throughout all history love proves itself to be the Almighty's final power, the final greatness of His heart, the last revelation of His Spirit.

> EBERHARD ARNOLD, *Innenland*,
> "The Experience of God"

August 26

We will not enter the kingdom of heaven through good intentions; we will enter only by becoming truly changed men. We must become different altogether in order to fit into the kingdom of heaven. Otherwise we cannot enter. God can take us into the kingdom of heaven only if we become children. Our attitude to God must be such that we no longer have in us the innate opposition to Him, but break with it.

CHRISTOPH BLUMHARDT, *Blumhardt Calendar*

August 27

If you want freedom, then believe in Jesus as the one who came from above. Believe in Him and His mercy. Hold firmly to Him, and with Him crush everything satanic within yourself. Believe that we have a Savior who is victor over all that holds men in such bondage and slavery. Believe it and hold to Him, and you will discover that He is the one who frees you and all creation from every servitude.

JOHANN CHRISTOPH BLUMHARDT, *Blumhardt Calendar*

August 28

The planet earth is surrounded, as it were, by an insulating layer formed by the thoughts of men, by the mass-impulses of men. And now it is important for God's Spirit, for God's love, that somewhere there is a breach, that somewhere absolute love, full brotherliness and complete clarity, also complete readiness for the fight against all evil spirits, can break through and break in. It makes no difference where this place is. One could say it is neither here nor there. Just as the clouds in the sky change continually, thus also this open place through which God's love and peace break in is not bound to any one place. Jesus says that where two or three gather in His name, in His being, in His power, He is in their midst.

EBERHARD ARNOLD, spoken in a meeting, Sept. 1935

August 29

The hour of decision has come over the world; even the blind must see it! Therefore it is important now to get together, not for our sake, but the Ark is meant, that it may reach the shore and lay the foundations for a new world. It is meant in the sense that we belong wherever there is the seed of a new world, where the light of peace and of unity has broken in through the dark layers which surround the world. All must come together and remain together, for it is the hour of decision, and no disunion can be tolerated. It is a matter of life or death, of love or hatred, of God or Satan.

> EBERHARD ARNOLD, spoken in a meeting, Sept. 1935

August 30

Nothing is needed more today than love. Nothing is needed more today than unity in love. This abundant, complete, absolute oneness, which permits no thwarting and no disturbing of the unity in which we become one heart and one soul, is needed today more than perhaps at any other time. Just that is most needed from God, the opposite of which has been lashed into greatest fury by the demons. Certainly propertylessness is very much needed today; certainly it is of greatest significance that there be purity in men's lives, complete abstinence and asceticism before marriage and absolute faithfulness in marriage in the sense that everything which takes place does so out of the Spirit.

> EBERHARD ARNOLD, spoken in a meeting, Sept. 1935

August 31

Peace is in opposition to fear. Peace is the unity of divine life, and as such it overcomes fear of the disintegration of death.

Only perfect life has no end. A short period is appointed for all that is mortal and all the efforts of mortals. Only the peace of God and the kingdom of His Prince of Peace, who rose from the dead, know no end. The work of man must yield to the work of God. Where His lordship extends, peace knows no end.

> EBERHARD ARNOLD, *Innenland*, "The Peace of God"

September 1

God wants to give the inner life an indestructible harmony which is to work outwardly in powerful melodies of love. This is the strength for activity which has its source in the energy of inner concentration.

> EBERHARD ARNOLD, *Innenland*, "The Inner Life"

September 2

The light drives away the rising mist. It destroys nothing. But when another world nears it, it quietly and almost imperceptibly drives out of that world all that it will not tolerate. Unless we draw near to the universal sun, all light remains extinguished for us.

> EBERHARD ARNOLD, *Innenland*,
> "Light and Fire"

September 3

My inner feeling urged me more and more to stand with those who represent social and pacifistic ethics. I recognized more and more clearly that the will of Jesus is stopped by no barriers or walls of public life.

> EBERHARD ARNOLD, from a letter,
> Feb. 1920

In our latest meetings here in Berlin we were concerned with the question of unreality. What most people call Utopia can become the most real and living thing in the life of a man.

> EBERHARD ARNOLD, from a letter,
> Mar. 1920

September 4

We shall reach the great end. It will not come all at once. It will come very quietly. One thing after another will come to an end in the world. One thing after another will no longer be tolerated. You can hardly imagine how great are the powers of God that can give men a new mind and a new heart, so that they themselves will get rid of all that stands in the way.

> Christoph Blumhardt, "I Am With You"

September 5

Without difficulties there is no victory. It is part of every cause of God that it has to go through troubles in order to attain the right maturity and capacity to achieve. Therefore let us stand firmly together in these things, and strengthen and help one another.

> Eberhard Arnold, from a letter, June 1920

September 6

Do you think the Son of Man will find faith in our time? ... With all our studying and investigating we have clogged up our hearts and heads to the point where we can no longer feel the immediate presence of Jesus Christ ... Yet to Jesus Christ belongs the victory today and tomorrow as also in the past: He has always been the victor over the dust.

  CHRISTOPH BLUMHARDT, "Our
  Human Right"

September 7

God is might and fire,
Apostle-might, apostle-fire,
Breaks the demon spell
And sweeps away the ghosts of hell.

God, thou Spirit and might,
The dead thou free'st from chasm's night;
Spirit, thou art Christ,
Forever circling earth and skies.

Spirit fills, breaks through;
He scales the walls of mountains high,
Brings the farthest nigh;
He brings refreshing wind to all.

  EBERHARD ARNOLD, 1923

September 8

The Church praises Him who became

man, who suffered and died and rose again, and overcame the kingdom of the underworld in His descent into hell. He is the strong, the mighty, the undying. He comes himself. He comes to the Church, attended by the armies of His angel princes. Thus heaven is opened for the believers. They hear and see the choir of singing angels. Through the coming of Christ to the Church in the presence of the power of the Spirit, the first historical coming of Christ and His future second coming are confirmed.

EBERHARD ARNOLD, *The Early Christians*

September 9

Whoever accepts God in Jesus, whoever receives in Him God's forgiveness and God's working, embraces God himself directly. God is contained in the faith of the heart. For God himself has gripped the heart. God never divides himself, however, when He imparts himself. He gives himself wholly. The keen awareness of one's own nothingness, of one's divided and sinful state—this awareness, which is truthfulness, makes it possible to receive the One who is infinitely different and eternally indivisible.

EBERHARD ARNOLD, *Innenland*,
"The Experience of God"

September 10

Faith is confronted by God's greatness as something so inviolable that man's petty power cannot possibly touch God. No human power that strives to unite with God can lead to this goal.

In a life which is active in public, faith expresses itself in helpful actions of love; this is brought about by God. In this new action of man, it is God who loves and acts.

EBERHARD ARNOLD, *Innenland*,
"The Experience of God"

September 11

"As my Father has loved me, so I have loved you," said I to my beloved disciples; and yet I send them out into the world not to have temporal joys, but to great conflicts; not to honor, but to contempt; not to idleness, but to labors; not to rest, but to bring forth much good fruit with patience. Remember well these words that I have spoken to you, for they are true and cannot be denied.

THOMAS A KEMPIS, *Imitation of Christ*

September 12

Sacrifice yourself for once for God's will. It will not be in vain. Sacrifice yourself for truth, for justice. Sacrifice yourself for once against all human sense for something that is truly good. Sacrifice yourself for Christ in all things. Seek the virtues of the kingdom of God. There is a very great strength in it. If we want to have joy in Christ, an unbroken joy, then we must learn this self-sacrifice. Things will never be better in the world unless self-sacrificing people offer themselves as workers. Stand for something; then your joy will be lasting. Then there will be light and all men will rejoice when the battle is won for the honor of God.

CHRISTOPH BLUMHARDT, "Joy in the Lord"

September 13

As in the whole of nature, God breaks into the history of men in mighty power whenever terrifying horrors shake humanity. Empires and world powers are the instruments of the force of wrath whenever God's greatness strikes the nations to earth. All nations of the world must be brought to the point where they fall at the feet of the God of all worlds.

EBERHARD ARNOLD, *Innenland*,
"The Experience of God"

September 14

The experience of God runs through all of human history as the overpowering of man by God's overwhelming superiority. The first experience of God by human awe and reverence is His tremendous might, before which all men's powers are nothing.

God is unattainably high and glorious. Thus the prophets know that no other power can endure beside Him.

EBERHARD ARNOLD, *Innenland*,
"The Experience of God"

September 15

He is speaking to the North, "O come!"
He is calling to the South, "Withhold no more."
Come, O come, to where the King is calling,
Sending out a wind to wake the sleepers and the poor.

In the tumult of a world of steel,
There's a whisper of a wind upon the street.
Rise, and come, though long and hard the
    journey,
Yonder is the city where the South and
    North shall meet.

    PHILIP BRITTS, 1941

September 16

The childlike man does not experience God's power and greatness without nature. He cannot disregard creation when he stands before the Creator. In the mysterious relationships of the created worlds, the believing creature senses the might of the Creator which gives greatness, life, coherence and unity to all things created.

    EBERHARD ARNOLD, *Innenland*,
    "The Experience of God"

September 17

Through the experience of God, man is drawn into the end of creation. The fiery baptism of God's judgment wants to revive the phoenix from the ashes. The dying of the old world heralds the beginning of the new. When the human heart is touched by God, it is close to death because life is coming to it. The death of Christ brings the resurrection.

EBERHARD ARNOLD, *Innenland*,
"The Experience of God"

September 18

It is the deathly loneliness of the Crucified that frees us from our own importance. It is the step into death by faith that leads us through the grave to the certainty of life. Christ has accepted me so utterly that He becomes united with me and says, "I am this poor sinner; that is, all his sin and death is my sin and my death." In this unity unto death we are freed from all sin, in spite of the most frightening awareness of sin. We gain life in the Risen One.

EBERHARD ARNOLD, *Innenland*,
"The Experience of God"

September 19

Peace is born of thoughts of the good. In the strength of peace one wants the good for all men and all things. A heart that thinks evil cheats itself and all others of peace. It becomes unhappy and spreads unhappiness. But he who works towards peace through the good, brings the joy of life to men.

EBERHARD ARNOLD, *Innenland*,
"The Peace of God"

September 20

Peace is the work of God. Without the Creator there is no peace in the creation. Just as there can be no outer peace without the inner peace of social justice, just as there can be no justice without the community of creative work, so there can be no peace without God. God alone is love. Only the active working of His Spirit of love creates peace.

EBERHARD ARNOLD, *Innenland*,
"The Peace of God"

September 21

Envy and strife are the marks of folly, of a worldly, emotional and devilish wisdom, bringing only disorder and evil. The wisdom which comes from God brings peace; for it is full of good deeds of mercy.

The message of peace means the fighting task of conquering all lands through the weapons of the Spirit, and subjecting them to God's lordship. It is for this task alone that the King and Commander of Peace wills to be with us.

EBERHARD ARNOLD, *Innenland*,
"The Peace of God"

September 22

If we seek God's kingdom and leave the temporal behind without looking into it too much; if we look into the kingdom of our God and Savior; then our senses will be opened and our innermost being—which is after all the most important—will receive open windows through which the light of the Eternal can fall. Then we shall be the most blest of men.

CHRISTOPH BLUMHARDT, *Blumhardt Calendar*

September 23

I give you the Lord's assurance that you may expect the forgiveness of your sins with complete confidence. The more certain this forgiveness is, the less you must go on discussing the past. It does you harm if you speak about it again and again. From now on leave it completely alone, as if it had not happened at all. In this way you do honor to the mercy given you; for this mercy must be recognized, and not doubted over and over again or felt to be uncertain. For the rest, what you must do is to remain in the fear of the Lord, yet look to Him with joy and courage!

JOHANN CHRISTOPH BLUMHARDT,
Blumhardt Calendar

September 24

Christ, who is undivided, wants to have us whole and undivided. He loves decision. He loves His enemies more than His half-hearted friends. He hates those who falsify Him more than those who oppose Him. What He abhors is the lukewarm, the colorless gray, the half-light, the pious talk that blurs and mixes everything and commits one to nothing. He sweeps all this away whenever He draws near.

EBERHARD ARNOLD, *Innenland*,
"The Peace of God"

September 25

Yes, Jesus is the Victor;
Believing, we shall fight.
As through the dark thy light shall lead,
We follow, Jesus, thee.
For all the world shall to Him bow
Till silenced is His every foe.
Yes, Jesus conquers all!

JOHANN CHRISTOPH BLUMHARDT

September 26

Under the marvelous protection of good powers we await confidently what may come. God is with us in the evening and in the morning and with absolute certainty in each new day.

God must be acknowledged in the midst of life. In life and not only in death; in health and strength and not only in suffering; in action, not only in sin, God wants to be recognized.

DIETRICH BONHOEFFER, executed by Hitler, April 1945. From poems written in prison.

September 27

When we are called to follow Christ, we are summoned to an exclusive attachment to His person. The grace of His call bursts all the bonds of legalism. It is a gracious call, a gracious commandment. It transcends the difference between the law and the Gospel. Christ calls, the disciple follows; that is grace and commandment in one. "I will walk at liberty, for I seek thy commandments." (Psalm 119, 45)

> DIETRICH BONHOEFFER, *The Cost of Discipleship*

September 28

Are you worried because you find it so hard to believe? No one should be surprised at the difficulty of faith, if there is some part of his life where he is consciously resisting or disobeying the commandment of Jesus. Is there some part of your life which you are refusing to surrender at His behest, some sinful passion, maybe, or some animosity, some hope, perhaps your ambition or your reason? If so, you must not be surprised that you have not received the Holy Spirit, that prayer is difficult, or that your request for faith remains unanswered ... The man who disobeys cannot believe, for only he who obeys can believe.

DIETRICH BONHOEFFER, *The Cost of Discipleship*

September 29

Jesus wants men to understand Him as the boundless love of God, and in this love He wants to conquer; in this love He wants to be the flame in which we burn ourselves pure, because judgment must be. We have to be judged and things have to be put to rights. But it is God's love and God's mercy alone that puts us through His judgment to set us free from everything that enslaves us and makes us miserable people now, people who live today, and tomorrow disappear in the darkness of death. Take me for a witness like that, and the testimony of all the men of God who have been born in Jesus Christ will back me up.

CHRISTOPH BLUMHARDT, "The Day of God's Love"

September 30

Only one thing matters: to be open to the living God, to the life-giving Spirit of

Jesus Christ, so that He may awaken and bring into being the same life that He gave to the early Christians. If we are open in this way, new unities of life will constantly arise in which the love of complete community encompasses and penetrates everything. Complete community is a matter of new birth and resurrection. This has been given even to our time by the Holy Spirit of Jesus Christ in the power of eternal birth and new resurrection.

EBERHARD ARNOLD, *Innenland*, "The Holy Spirit"

October 1

It is the will toward God, the will to the all-controlling might of His kingdom, His love and justice, which forces us into the inner seclusion where the loneliness of the soul becomes the fellowship of the soul with God and the fellowship of the Church.

EBERHARD ARNOLD, *Innenland*, "The Inner Life"

October 2

As soon as the bustling activity of our self, which wilfully pervades external things, no longer stands in our light and obscures it, we see God directly before our innermost hearts. God proves himself to us as the radiant sun which alone can bring enduring life. He leads on the new day, His day, which judges the darkness of the life of self, and seeks to redeem each individual to the light and unite all under His sway.

EBERHARD ARNOLD, *Innenland*,
"The Inner Life"

October 3

Just as the earth would be no less dead than the moon but for its glowing depths—just as the inner core contains the vital strength of a fruit—just as the beautiful chalice-like petals of a flower hold the organs of its fertilization hidden within it —in the same way there can be but one center for all vital energy: that which is within and hidden.

EBERHARD ARNOLD, *Innenland*,
"The Inner Life"

October 4

It is depressing to see how blunt everything still is, how little we come to a holy revolution, how little we fight the battle until death, how little we dare to break with all existing values toward that which is to come! I do wish that you may dare the utmost. The utmost begins with the free decision to fight against oneself, to give up oneself, to place one's very small self into the very great for which alone it is worth living. May Christ be your deliverer and leader in this!

EBERHARD ARNOLD, from a letter, March 1925

October 5

In speaking before others, it is possible for a great miracle to happen. God, really God, works so powerfully that speakers and listeners no longer feel anything that comes from men, especially from the one speaking, whom they forget completely. They are so overpowered by God that chains fall, sickness departs, new birth is given and God and His Kingdom alone prevail.

EBERHARD ARNOLD, from a letter, July 1925

October 6

It must have been difficult for you to see so much break down under God's flashes of lightning, to have to recognize so much as inadequate, yes, some of it even as dangerous and destructive! Not only that which is evil, also that which is almost good, must yield to what is better, what is alone and truly good.

EBERHARD ARNOLD, from a letter, 1934

October 7

How wonderful are the inner experiences of many in this dreadful time of war. In the midst of hell the eternal power of the kingdom of heaven has shown itself. Basically it is like this everywhere in our lives. In our hearts, in our work, everywhere, we are surrounded by hellish powers. Again and again, in spite of the prevailing conditions, we must keep watch over the kingdom of God.

EBERHARD ARNOLD, from a letter, Mar. 1920

October 8

Many times the Savior calls out to us, "Watch! . . . Watch for my future, for the

future of Jesus Christ!" With this call the
Lord Jesus gives us a task. It is a blessed,
an important task. If we fulfil this task,
it is as though His future were coming into
our present time.

      CHRISTOPH BLUMHARDT, "The
      Savior Is Coming!"

October 9

The earth prepared for that great hour,
And all that lives within thy power
Lives on in high rejoicing.
Because the world of God so great
For thy Kingdom didst thou create,
Thou comest to renew us.

Now blows the wind, and sighs do play;
A star is clear. How far away?
A sign it is, unfailing.
So see we thy eternal light
That burns into our age, our night,
And we with it are burning.

      OTTO SALOMON, Sannerz, 1921

October 10

Jesus Christ is the revelation of God—
of the God who in this revelation of His

nature is the healer of the sick and of sinners. Whoever receives His Spirit and becomes a new man through his new birth is free, certain, open-hearted, clear and open-eyed. He is in possession of a power which enables him to fulfil the most difficult and impracticable tasks, even to do the impossible.

EBERHARD ARNOLD, *The Early Christians*

October 11

In the Church of the Spirit the believer's heart is made pure and free from every deadly sin of selfish life, by community with the death of Christ. His heart is directed in righteousness towards God and His uniting kingdom. His body knows that he has been cleansed from deathly lusts in the baptism of faith. He stands in the unity of God's life, in the certainty of God's promise and assurance of perpetual life.

EBERHARD ARNOLD

October 12

God sent the Spirit of His Son into human hearts. This means obligation and authority; it means that all men who are gripped by this Spirit expel all other spirits from their entire sphere of life.

The Spirit of unity wants community in all things. This spirit brings about unity among men, because it brings men into unity with God.

EBERHARD ARNOLD, *Innenland*,
"The Experience of God"

October 13

The peace that reigns in human hearts as God's unity makes men bearers and builders of universal peace. All spirits of unpeace, of war and civil war, the spirits of competition and property, are banished by the Church of God.

EBERHARD ARNOLD, *Innenland*,
"The Experience of God"

October 14

Joy in God's love fills believing hearts to overflowing, so much that their love has to go out to all men. All men shall become the object of this joyful faith; one after the other they are to be encompassed by love and the perfect community of love. The spirit of justice and peace and joy is the Spirit of the Church.

> EBERHARD ARNOLD, *Innenland*,
> "The Experience of God"

October 15

The peace of God is a force like a streaming flood, a reviving wind, an almighty power. It alone can bring all the mills of human work into action. It can be compared to a mighty torrent whose waters overflow, while the overwhelming power and movement of its depths perform the greatest task.

> EBERHARD ARNOLD, *Innenland*,
> "The Experience of God"

October 16

To those who have great trust in the Lord Jesus, He can also give great mercy, great strength, great endurance unto death. He can provide for them and care for them. When they are wounded He can heal them. When they grieve He can comfort them. When they must taste the terrors of death He can give them life.

> CHRISTOPH BLUMHARDT, *Blumhardt Calendar*

October 17

In all our corruption and frailty we must live for eternity, as the Savior teaches us. We must renounce everything in order to attain eternity. The evil that is on earth cannot harm us, because we are allowed to live in the eternal life. But we must have faith. God must really be our refuge and our hope; otherwise we will be lost.

CHRISTOPH BLUMHARDT, *Blumhardt Calendar*

October 18

The cross is laid on every Christian. The first Christ-suffering which every man must experience is the call to abandon the attachments of this world. It is that dying of the old man which is the result of his encounter with Christ. As we embark upon discipleship we surrender ourselves to Christ in union with His death; we give over our lives to death. Thus it begins; the cross is not the terrible end to an otherwise God-fearing and happy life, but it meets us at the beginning of our communion with Christ.

DIETRICH BONHOEFFER, *The Cost of Discipleship*

October 19

We can of course shake off the burden which is laid upon us, but only find that we have a still heavier burden to carry—a yoke of our own choosing, the yoke of our self. But Jesus invites all who travail and are heavy laden to throw off their own yoke and take His yoke upon them—and His yoke is easy, and His burden is light . . . Under His yoke we are certain of his nearness and communion. It is He whom the disciple finds as he lifts up his cross.

DIETRICH BONHOEFFER, *The Cost of Discipleship*

October 20

Men who have been gripped by God can only look upon all transitory inequalities as a rousing incitement to the brotherhood of perfect love.

The same need, indebtedness and insignificance made them all "poor", as they liked to be called, especially in the earliest epoch, because their faith in the one God and their attitude to material goods could only be understood as poverty.

EBERHARD ARNOLD, *The Early Christians*

October 21

We may have heard and read a great deal about the words and life of Jesus. We may be able to say a great deal about the words of the Bible. But unless the spirit and essence of His love grips and encompasses the whole of our lives to the depths, dead knowledge only leads to destruction.

EBERHARD ARNOLD, *Innenland*,
"The Experience of God"

October 22

Experience of God means strength for action. There is no love that does not live in deeds. The experience of God, because it is the life of love, is also an experiencing of strength.

If the substance of faith is Jesus Christ, then this faith must be just as active in His perfect love as He was. Personally and actually, the believer must represent and carry out the same that Jesus achieved.

EBERHARD ARNOLD, *Innenland*,
"The Experience of God"

October 23

Peace is born when the body of justice

is brought to the light. The Church of Jesus Christ is the organism of this body in justice, peace and joy of the Spirit.

At the given time justice shall arise. With the rising of the sun the day of great peace breaks. In Jesus the day has dawned. It comes anew in Christ. Peace is guaranteed when justice arises resplendent.

EBERHARD ARNOLD, *Innenland*,
"The Peace of God"

October 24

The experience of God is the love that conquers all opposition. It is the strength of the new creation. It is the spirit of God's coming dominion. It is the unique element of the new structure. It is the herald of the new time. It is the organic power of unity. It is the building up of the new humanity.

In the Church of Jesus Christ, God is experienced. In the Church of complete love, God's Spirit brings Christ's kingdom of perfect justice to the earth. The experience of God means the rulership of God in the Church of Jesus Christ.

EBERHARD ARNOLD, *Innenland*,
"The Experience of God"

October 25

As long as we withdraw from the completeness of the whole, as long as we in a small-minded way put what is individual and isolated in the foreground, we are torn by untruthfulness and confusion. We are in conflict. We lose ourselves in superficialities. We persist in folly. We remain in death.

EBERHARD ARNOLD, *Innenland*,
"The Peace of God"

October 26

What a great thing is the faith in the living God who can create something even out of nothing! But who has this faith? Present-day mankind seems more and more to be inwardly dead. Who can still have hope for something to come out of this void? Yet just as Jesus arose from the dead, so will mankind also rise up again from its spiritual deadness through God's might.

JOHANN CHRISTOPH BLUMHARDT,
Blumhardt Calendar

October 27

What are you Christians here for? For

nothing else but to proclaim God's kingdom. You are here to try to give the kingdom of God to men. In this unjust world you are to stand with faith and courage and endurance and say, "It must come; I will give up my life rather than swerve from this goal." This is your purpose as Christians.

CHRISTOPH BLUMHARDT, *Blumhardt Calendar*

October 28

Marriage, this is what I call the resolve of two to create a unity which is more than those who created it. I call marriage reverence for one another and for the fulfilment of such a resolve.

You must love this land of children, and this love must be your nobility.

Faith as the power of truth which clarifies and frees from confusion, is the character of true marriage.

Freedom does not demand intoxication or blindness, but power and clarity.

Love opens up paradise.

EBERHARD ARNOLD, "On the Struggle of Young People in the Problem of Love"

October 29

True community of marriage can move only from unity of spirit through the emotional into the physical. It can live, therefore, only in faithfulness, only and solely in steadfast, everlasting unity. This is possible only under the rulership of the Spirit. Only out of this can physical purity be desired. Only when the emotions are ruled by the Spirit can freeing and purification become reality.

> EBERHARD ARNOLD, "On the Struggle of Young People in the Problem of Love"

October 30

The discipline of God's Church is the most careful marriage chastity. First and foremost it means unstained purity before marriage and outside of marriage. Yet also in a very serious and definite way this discipline means the right mutual choice of spouses, on the basis of their natural but even more their spiritual calling for one another. One marries the one human being who is destined for one from eternity.

> EBERHARD ARNOLD, *Innenland*, "The Conscience and Its Witness"

October 31

The all-embracing Spirit is the unity of all freed spirits. He effects the freedom of the soul's powers, which now flow toward one another, without remaining dependent on sympathy or antipathy, on the states of the body. The Spirit dominates the uniting of men, and takes into His sphere all material goods.

Where freedom, purity and the love of God reign; where Christ lives in the individuals; where His Spirit unfolds all gifts and powers, there grows a living unity which can only be seen as one body.

EBERHARD ARNOLD, "Love-Life and Love"

November 1

Through unity with the eternal powers we must gain the strength of character to be tested in the stream of the world, the strength which alone can cope with the demands of the age. Not escape, but concentration for the attack, is the watchword.

EBERHARD ARNOLD, *Innenland*, "The Inner Life"

November 2

It is comforting that Jesus does not say, "I am your light," or "I am the light of a nation," or "I am the light of a church," or even "I am the light of my disciples." No, He says, "I am the light of the world." It is as though He wanted to say to us, "Don't draw me into all your everyday, petty affairs. Don't draw me into your own nature. Nobody should think that I have come only to him. No, accept me as the one who has come into the world, through whom the world has been created."

CHRISTOPH BLUMHARDT, "The Light of the World"

November 3

Dear Father in heaven, give us thy Spirit, so that something of thee may be manifest on earth, and not only what is human. Let divine power and divine truth be with us in all our doing. Let us always remain strong of heart, so that thou art around us even when it becomes dark; then powers of peace and of salvation will be revealed in us. Thou canst achieve everything, also things that we do not understand, and thou helpest us in everything. We cannot do what thou canst do. Therefore we have hope and faith that thou wilt possess our whole lives with thy might and the lives of the many people who sigh in their hearts for the genuine truth of life. Amen.

CHRISTOPH BLUMHARDT, *Blumhardt Calendar*

November 4

Watch and pray, the Lord Jesus is coming! This watching is part of our lives, of our service to God. The Savior urges us seriously to "Watch, watch, watch!" . . . It is as though He were always waiting and asking, "How can I come closer to this person, to that person? How can I meet this one who is waiting for me? How can I go to meet many at a time, so that again and again new victories are given?"

CHRISTOPH BLUMHARDT, "The Savior is Coming"

November 5

In anguished grief groan men, divided all,
Though wholeness seeking, yet their hearts
    are ruled
By spirits, powers that separate, enslave.

When cometh unity, the Kingdom of
　Peace?
We come and plead the Spirit from the
　heights
That formed in us a holy Church might be.
Bring blazing fire, lives broken, now as one
In thy great love. O Lord, come thou soon!

  Else von Hollander, 1925

November 6

 God went out from himself. He has truly revealed himself in His Word, in the creation which came to pass through His Word, in the incarnation of His Word, and in His Spirit of truth and unity. God has opened His heart. He has come forth from himself. He has turned toward us. He has revealed His thoughts to us. He has revealed His essence and His will to us. We little, weak beings are the object of His concern.

  Eberhard Arnold, "The Meaning and Power of Prayer Life"

November 7

 Only those hearts have peace and only those people bring peace and cause peace who love the whole truth. The truth of God brings wisdom and genuineness, for it creates perfect love. Love is ultimate truth. It brings peace.

Love, as the peace of God, is the bond of perfection that unites in complete surrender and common activity all that was broken and scattered.

> EBERHARD ARNOLD, *Innenland*,
> "The Peace of God"

November 8

Without the final future that we are awaiting, the whole of Christianity would really be nothing. If only our hearts were completely gripped by this! Surely after the unbelievably horrible and alarming news we have heard, we should all stretch out our hands toward what is to come. Let us ask that at last the world may be redeemed from all the horrors, and the dawn of the new day may break, even though the darkness of judgment must precede it.

> EBERHARD ARNOLD, "The Expectation of That Which is to Come"

November 9

We are here together in a memorable moment of history. We feel how the demonic powers are storming at us from all sides to shake the Church, like autumn storms rushing through the woods. Yet all the more we feel the original power of the living tree that is Jesus Christ, this tree of life of His Church. We feel this unconquerable power about which the Shepherd of Hermas says that in the midst of winter it persists as the flourishing strength of the Church. In this wintertime we are awaiting what is to come.

EBERHARD ARNOLD, "Healing and Expectation"

November 10

How is the disciple to know what kind of cross is meant for him? He will find out as soon as he begins to follow his Lord and to share His life.

Who is pure in heart? Only those who have surrendered their hearts completely to Jesus that He may reign in them alone. Only those whose hearts are undefiled by their own evil—and by their own virtues too.

> Dietrich Bonhoeffer, *The Cost of Discipleship*

November 11

Whether man knows it or not, the eternal is his only happiness; it makes him strong in the midst of the earthly, which bears the stamp of the temporal and has no eternity. All the hope that we have in our lives and for our lives, everything that is bright and brings joy, is connected with the name of Jesus. For He is the unique heavenly treasure which the Father in heaven gives to men. Thus our years on earth will be sheltered in the heavenly, if we become partakers in the name of Jesus.

> *Blumhardt Calendar*

November 12

Anyone who suffers with Christ and is willing to feel the pain without consolation so that he may test himself, will come through all the guilt and all its spikes and thorns which pierce deeply into his flesh and stir up his whole soul; he will come through all this to Jesus; he will come to His Advent. He must not say, "Oh, if only Jesus would come!" Our God will come and judge all the world, and He will judge me first of all because I give myself up to this judgment. Then the real meaning of the words, "He who overcomes shall inherit all things," will be experienced. Then the world will shine forth in the life of the Savior.

CHRISTOPH BLUMHARDT, "Thoughts of Advent"

November 13

For those nights when the sky is clouded a bright lantern is put into the wanderer's hand: the Word of God which lights the dark way ahead until the day begins and the morning star rises.

EBERHARD ARNOLD, *Innenland*, "Light and Fire"

November 14

The Savior is on the way. He is not quietly sitting somewhere in eternity, waiting for a certain moment when He will suddenly plunge in. He is on the way. We may at all times have His future before our eyes. We may expect it every day.

>   Christoph Blumhardt, "The Savior is Coming"

November 15

Watch, for the Savior is on the way! Watch for the world, too. Do not give the world up as though it were lost for all eternity. It is true that Jesus Christ's future brings separation. A judgment lies in the fact that one person can come to faith and to the joy in God, while another remains outside for the time being. But this should not trouble us. The future of Jesus Christ is and will be a great and powerful help in all situations for all men.

>   Christoph Blumhardt, "The Savior is Coming"

November 16

Yes, He comes, no longer far,
Soon will shine our Morning Star!
Soon will night be left behind!
Now the Savior of mankind
To our hearts will entrance find.

Fire, light! So shall it be,
Promise of His radiancy;
But the day will surely dawn
When the world will be His own,
Come to us, Lord Jesus Christ!

>   OTTO SALOMON, 1921

November 17

The peace of Christmas depends upon the freedom of obedience. The soil of birth bears peace. Mary believed. She obeyed. The Spirit came. Christ was born! Mary heard the Word and kept it in her heart.

>   EBERHARD ARNOLD, *Innenland*,
>   "The Peace of God"

God's kingdom came in Jesus to forsaken men of a world grown cold, in Jesus its King anointed by the Holy Spirit.

>   EBERHARD ARNOLD, *Innenland*,
>   "The Holy Spirit"

November 18

To sail through deadly peril,
Imprisoned by dark fate;
With multitudes to voyage,
By mortal powers racked;

Despairing, without mercy,
Condemned to utter gloom,
Is ruin without rescue.
The passage way is blocked.

There from the distant shore blinks
A light, an eye, a star!
He calls from shore to vessel,
He strikes the inmost heart.
The call wakes life from deadness,
It stirs the depths of birth.
Limbs lifeless, now arising,
Take up life's bond anew.

EBERHARD ARNOLD, 1925/26

November 19

The peace of Jesus Christ carries the non-violent battle of complete rulership of the Spirit into all the world against the power of the bloody sword. He who sees the King of Peace enters His kingdom in unsullied peace, even though like Him he must wade through the terrifying stream of death.

EBERHARD ARNOLD, *Innenland*,
"The Peace of God"

November 20

The dreadful birth pains of recent times are part of the curse of death which the loss of mankind's first peace has brought with it. Until the last judgment has taken place upon unpeace, until the terror-bringing unpeace has borne its last monstrous child, God's peace of the great Advent cannot be born. Immediately before the new breaks in, all the old must be shattered by the extremest need.

EBERHARD ARNOLD, *Innenland*,
"The Peace of God"

November 21

I know that Christ is in the flesh. Should I then have fear and say, "I am a sinner"? No! For then Christ would not be in the flesh. If I have to fear my own sin, then Christ did not come into the flesh. I fear no sin, no death. Christ came into this flesh, in which sin and death dwell. Therefore I am free! The victory is on my side, it is on your side. Only believe it, carry it in your hearts. Nothing else is needed. You need not appear to be better men now. If a man lives in the knowledge that Jesus is now in the flesh, then everything else will come by itself.

CHRISTOPH BLUMHARDT, "Christ in the Flesh"

November 22

In the flame of the Spirit there is living unity between those who have gone and those who remain on earth. The unanimity of the people gathered to full community in the house of God is the unity of the Church above, living in that perfect light to which no mortal life of our earth's shadow has access.

>   EBERHARD ARNOLD, *Innenland*,
>   "Light and Fire"

November 23

God's fire of wrath becomes a basis for His pitying love, that is, for the light in His heart. In the decisive times of His judgment His love is to be made manifest. In the fullness of God's time the last judgment becomes the culmination of His reign of love.

>   EBERHARD ARNOLD, *Innenland*,
>   "Light and Fire"

November 24

Against the powers of death and hell we cry out today in all simplicity, "Jesus is victor!" We cannot think it over too much. It is no concern of ours how it is to come about. But one thing we have seen: The foundation on which we live has been undermined; Jesus is victor!

CHRISTOPH BLUMHARDT, *Blumhardt Calendar*

November 25

God's illumination approaches with elemental power. Unforgettable are the moments when a bright flash of lightning lays bare the deep, black cloak of night, discloses every hiding place and brings to light all the vermin of darkness.

EBERHARD ARNOLD, *Innenland*, "Light and Fire"

November 26

We can not say for the mass of mankind that the day of the Son of Man has come. We await this still. But waiting demands great strength. No one can bear it if the bright light of Christ has not risen within him. This waiting is a tremendous thing. The power of expectancy must penetrate darkness, death and the most chaotic tumult, with the day of the Son of Man. This is no fantasy. These beams of power produced in our awaiting should pierce the world's darkness so that men feel it although they may never realize whence it comes. It is of tremendous importance that expectation is a power not only for us, but for others too.

November 27

The illuminating rays of the Lord of Light bring about the experience of Him. In the light the inward eye sees Him as He is. In the coming world of light all life and activity will be transformed into His clarity.

EBERHARD ARNOLD, *Innenland*,
"Light and Fire"

November 28

We should and can be ever alert and watchful. Jesus Christ's future must become your personal experience. Whenever you experience protection and remarkable help, whenever you are led on new ways and see others being led on new ways, you should think, "This is a piece of Jesus Christ's future . . . However poor we may be, however weak we may feel, we want to continue hoping and watching."

CHRISTOPH BLUMHARDT, "The Savior is Coming"

November 29

Made alive and awake through Christ's redemption, we shall have eyes that remain alert to see how God comes and what kingdom He brings.

EBERHARD ARNOLD, from a letter, July 1934

November 30

Please—yes, I beg you most urgently; bear your great, sacred responsibility steadfastly, like a burning light in your hands. For the sake of this warming, radiating light, do not let yourselves be pushed or shaken or even knocked over! Then the fullness of your burning candles will send its light over to me as in a Christmas vision, and will strengthen me and bring me back. . . . You know that the incarnation of the Creator and His word of love, and Jesus' word and work in the outpouring of His

Spirit, is the strength in which you can do everything.

> EBERHARD ARNOLD, from a letter, November 1930

December 1

God's kingdom is approaching over all the earth. God is near wherever the complete transformation of all things which His reign brings with it, is sought. His kingdom has no bounds in space.

> EBERHARD ARNOLD, *Innenland*, "The Inner Life"

December 2

We are heralds of the last kingdom. We stand here and go out as bearers of the cause, as envoys, as messengers of God's kingdom. The turning of all things is near; everything else must be overthrown, God's love alone shall triumph!

> EBERHARD ARNOLD, from a letter, July 1934

December 3

The shining glory of awakening life is terribly painful for all those who are estranged from the strong light. Because they are accustomed to the prevailing darkness, the blazing radiance becomes unbearable torture for them. It burns in their eyes like fire. The victorious light becomes judgment. The shining flame of the life which demands love judges the darkness of unpeace and puts to flight the coldness of injustice.

EBERHARD ARNOLD, *Innenland*, "Light and Fire"

December 4

Man born on earth comes into the darkness. But when he hears the Gospel, a light from Jesus Christ comes into him, a light of life. Then he can no longer stay in the world's darkness. Then he must come out, straight out into the light, into eternity. So we live in the darkness and yet are in the light. So we live in affliction and yet live in joy. We live under a burden and yet we have wings to go to meet God, the eternal light and life of all creation.

CHRISTOPH BLUMHARDT, *Blumhardt Calendar*

December 5

Justice will save the world. Rejoice! The heavens say, Rejoice! The angels say, Rejoice! A new word, "And God spoke!" sounds in our hearts today. Hear it, rejoice, exult. Joy is coming, truth is coming, life is coming, justice is coming over the world. The darkness must be dispersed, struggles will cease, because Jesus Christ, the Prince of Justice, is coming out of God's kingdom to us!

CHRISTOPH BLUMHARDT, *Blumhardt Calendar*

December 6

A dear God is much pleasanter than a holy God, a just God, a true God. But here we must and shall distinguish. Let us look up to the God who has founded His kingdom in the name of our Lord Jesus Christ, who is a King of all kings and a Lord of all lords. Let us love His kingdom, His justice, His holy name. Let us love His holiness above everything. Let us say to ourselves until we are used to it and have it in our flesh and blood: Holy, holy, holy is our God!

CHRISTOPH BLUMHARDT, *Blumhardt Calendar*

December 7

The Christ-Spirit which works everywhere became the Son of Man in Jesus. He was the kingtom of God on this earth. At the place He came to, the kingdom of God broke in. Where He lived, the powers of the future world were manifest. His words of personal forgiveness of sins were radiations of the future just as powerful as His acts of healing the sick and waking the dead, or as His proclamation of the future conditions of God's kingdom which were to transform all the conditions on this earth from the ground up.

EBERHARD ARNOLD, "Expectation"

December 8

He who puts his hand to God's plough looks forward. He lives only in the future. He who looks back and loses himself in historical scruples and in reveries of his own history, is not qualified for God's kingdom. When in bygone ages people longed for God's kingdom, they were expecting the same Christ whom we must expect today. The Word became flesh.

EBERHARD ARNOLD, "Expectation"

December 9

The expectation of what is to come, which is as all-embracing as it is unshakably certain, cannot be a passive waiting in which one is occupied in a sweetish and soft way with oneself and one's own small circle of like-minded people. No, this expectation is divine power. This expectation means the uniting with the powers of the future. It means the inward uniting with the character of the future world.

EBERHARD ARNOLD, "Expectation"

December 10

The expectation of the Coming One is the religious certainty that the divine must conquer the demonic, love must conquer hate, the all-embracing must conquer the isolated. Certainty tolerates no limitation. God embraces everything. When we trust in Him for the future, we trust for the present. The Advent hope is a certainty of faith which must show itself in action as mutual responsibility for the whole of life.

EBERHARD ARNOLD, "Expectation"

December 11

The last prophet of the old time who was to precede the coming Christ was filled with the Holy Spirit when He was still unborn. His father and mother too became filled with the Holy Spirit for Him. Mary received the Spirit before Jesus' life began. In this same way the apostolic Church, which from the beginning of its way followed Jesus, was full of the Holy Spirit. "When they had prayed, the place where they were gathered was shaken, and all were filled with the Holy Spirit and spoke God's Word with joyful courage."

EBERHARD ARNOLD, *Innenland*, "The Holy Spirit"

December 12

The Church of the Spirit, born out of faith, is God's unity of the creative Spirit. Being this, the Church surpasses everything that is human. She has the power to rule and to determine the hearts of the believers. From the believing heart she carries peace into all the world. Like the birth of Christ, every calling of God's Church takes place in the unity of peace. Her ways are nothing but peace, just as peace among the peoples was and is and remains the purpose of Jesus Christ's whole working.

Eberhard Arnold, *Innenland*,
"The Peace of God"

December 13

Through every century runs the thread of the secret expectation of a coming age in which peace and justice shall reign; of a Kingdom whose ruler is yet unknown and which is of the highest mysterious order. There is no people on earth that has not carried this expectation deep in its heart. And now He has come in lowliness, in poverty, cast out from human society, in the feeding trough of a cow shed. Now He has come, the lowliest amongst the low. Now He came and was killed; for people did not want this witness to live.

Eberhard Arnold, "Expectation and Fulfilment"

December 14

Has this love been born in us, and has it been lived until death? Only if we are willing to take the message of this Son born of Mary so seriously as this—only then shall we belong to those who live in true expectation and who find something of true fulfilment.

> Eberhard Arnold, "Expectation and Fulfilment"

December 15

The Church is placed in this world in order to proclaim, in the midst of the heaviest darkness, this message: The Morning Star has risen in my heart, in our hearts, and soon will rise over the whole of the darkened world. Repent! Believe in the Gospel! He who is coming is near.

> Eberhard Arnold, "The Expectation of That Which Is to Come"

December 16

The God of the stars and their hosts, who will begin His rulership on earth, has laid His Spirit upon the One whose justice will never grow weary until it is firmly established over the whole earth as peace.

> Eberhard Arnold, *Innenland*, "The Peace of God"

December 17

Faith and love and hope in God demand something from us; for we recognize what God is and the love He has shown us through the birth of His Son. Our whole spirit demands that we speak up and say, "And yet—the night is far spent, the day is at hand!" This became true in the hour when Jesus was born on earth. It is true in God's eyes, and because it is true in His eyes we on earth must say in the name of Jesus Christ: It must become true on earth also; and because it must become true, it will become true. The night is far spent, the day is at hand!

>   CHRISTOPH BLUMHARDT, "The Day of God's Love"

December 18

God's love will never admit that there is anyone who is not loved. I say it boldly in the face of the whole world, in the face of heaven and the underworld: Everything is loved, because Jesus is born. All should feel that they are loved and not one single person should feel rejected—all are loved, because Jesus is born!

> CHRISTOPH BLUMHARDT, "The Day of God's Love"

December 19

To be a child of man
Down to the earth God came,
He came to make anew the life.
And death He came to conquer—
For this sang all creation
And earth and heaven rejoiced.

Then in all lands are loosened
The chains and bonds of evil,
Then breaketh every spell.
Light cometh into darkness,
The old rule then is shattered,
In glory comes His Kingdom.

> From an old Christmas song.

December 20

Not only has the Savior come; He will still come in God's glory in today's world. The future bears the name of Jesus Christ; it is our future and the future of the world, of all creation. The Savior is coming. He will reveal His glory and will help us, so that we may walk in His light, to His honor and praise.

JOHANN CHRISTOPH BLUMHARDT,
Blumhardt Calendar

December 21

And the Word became flesh, and dwelt among us, full of grace and truth; we have beheld his glory, glory as of the only Son from the Father.

Gospel of John, 1, 14

December 22

Wherever God's Word comes to a man, that which is eternal within him comes forth out of the pit and sees the divine in the light. This is something great. What is great in us is awakened through the Word which became flesh. Then a man changes, for his soul becomes alert and alive; his spirit arises from its slumber, and a longing for God comes to him. Man comes to himself. Man becomes completely different once his eyes are opened to see this glory. Truly one can say that unless a man's eyes are illumined in Jesus, he is altogether blind.

> JOHANN CHRISTOPH BLUMHARDT,
> *Blumhardt Calendar*

December 23

In these days of Christmas let us ask God that we may be ready. Let us ask God from our hearts that our hearts may be urged and moved again and again by God's good thoughts, by the greatest events; that we may think along big lines, not only in continents and planets, but in the cosmic constellations; that we may think not only in the cycles of years, but in decades, centuries and millennia, in the dimensions of God's thoughts, in the great lines of God. Let us not be a small generation which is met by great things! Let us be worthy, that we may be deemed worthy of a great time and a great calling!

> EBERHARD ARNOLD, Advent 1934

December 24

Christmas night! Oh, night of nights,
You make the very richest poor;
You send your light into all powers,
Make the dark night radiant bright.

Jesus is the light of lights,
Jesus is the strength of life!
Things beyond the world's belief
Jesus does for all His poor.

Make us poor, just as you were,
Jesus, poor through thy great love!
Make us weak, weak in thy strength;
Give thy pity in our need!

  EBERHARD ARNOLD, Christmas 1921

December 25

Peace is the flaming eye of the armies of God. It is the battle song of His heavenly hosts: "Glory to God in the highest! Peace on earth to men of good will." In the strength of this peace the Messiah-King entered the walls of Jerusalem. He rode no warhorse to a battle in which blood would be shed on both sides. The animal of poverty and peace bore Him as He was met by the cry, "Hail to Him who cometh in the name of the Lord. With Him is peace!"

  EBERHARD ARNOLD, *Innenland*,
"The Peace of God"

December 26

Wherever love proceeds from us and becomes truth, the time is fulfilled. Then the divine nature floods through all our human relationships and all our works. Then everything which today is lonely and scattered, and is seeking for the way of God, shall be bound together by divine power. Then, of human effort and of the divine miracle, shall that world be born in which Christmas is fulfilled as reality.

EBERHARD ARNOLD, "When the Time Was Fulfilled"

December 27

It was not after a great mass of people had completed something good, nor was it the successful result of any human efforts, that Christmas came. No; Christmas came as a miracle, as the child that comes when its time is fulfilled, as a gift of the Father which He lays into those arms that are stretched out in longing. In this way did Christmas come and always comes anew, both to individuals and to the whole world.

EBERHARD ARNOLD, "When the Time Was Fulfilled"

December 28

Because of the noise and activity of the struggle and the work, we often do not hear the hidden gentle sound and movement of the life that is coming into being. But here and there, at hours that are blessed, God lets us feel how He is at work everywhere and how His cause is growing and moving forwards. The time is being fulfilled and the light shall shine, perhaps just when it seems to us that the darkness is impenetrable.

> EBERHARD ARNOLD, "When the Time Was Fulfilled"

December 29

We have not come like Eastern kings
With gifts upon the pommel lying;
Our hands are empty and we came
Because we heard a baby crying.

We have not come like questing knights
With fiery swords and banners flying;
We heard a call and hurried here—
The call was like a baby crying.

But we have come with open hearts
From places where the torch is dying;
We seek a manger and a cross,
Because we heard a Baby crying.

> PHILIP BRITTS, 1939

December 30

The little stable in Bethlehem was the place where the love of God broke through. The mysterious men out of the East followed the Star and discovered the place of breaking-in, where the mystery of love lay in the helplessness of a human baby, wrapped in swaddling clothes in the feeding trough of an animal. They discovered the place where the love of God had broken through. That is the most important thing for every man, to discover in his own time and at his own hour the place where God's love has broken through, and then to follow the Star that has risen for him and to remain true to the light that has fallen into his heart.

> EBERHARD ARNOLD, spoken in a meeting, 1935

December 31

This year was one of richest grace
That thou in love didst give to me;
To paths of light thy hand has led,
In deepest joy my heart made free.

As offering to thy dear name
Oh, take my life in every part;
I give it thee complete and whole,
Fill thou alone my mind and heart.

Oh, may I live throughout the year
For thee alone, led by thy hand;
Protect me, Lord, from wrong and sin;
To serve thee purely here I stand.

EBERHARD ARNOLD, 1905

This is the end of all things: that Jesus appears with those who love Jesus. They will understand that the end is come in the establishment of the kingdom of God, in the wedding of the beloved Bridegroom and His Church.

This is the feast of joy of the City—the true Jerusalem — the united Church standing before the whole world as the embodiment of God's message:

The coming of Christ, His yearned-for reappearance, the longing call of the bride:

"Amen, yes, come, Lord Jesus!"

The second paragraph quoted for July 27 is from *The New Testament in Modern English*, copyright J. B. Phillips 1958. Used by permission of the Macmillan Company.

The two paragraphs for September 26 are translated from poems by Dietrich Bonhoeffer published in the volume *Widerstand und Ergebung*, and are used by permission of the Chr. Kaiser-Verlag, Muenchen.

Eight quotations from *The Cost of Discipleship* by Dietrich Bonhoeffer are used by permission of the Macmillan Company.

Passages for February 4, September 28, December 17 and December 18 are translated from *Ihr Menschen seid Gottes*, Vol. 3 of *Christoph Blumhardt: Eine Auswahl aus seinen Predigten, Andachten und Schriften*, edited by R. Lejeune; they are used by permission of the Rotapfel-Verlag, Zuerich. Other quotations from Christoph Blumhardt are translated from *Christoph Blumhardt und seine Botschaft*, by R. Lejeune, and are also used by permission of the Rotapfel-Verlag.

WITHDRAWN
from
Funderburg Library